Locked-Out Americans

Locked-Out Americans

A Memoir   John R. Fry

Harper & Row, Publishers
New York, Evanston, San Francisco, London

FIRST EDITION
STANDARD BOOK NUMBER: 06–063073–6
LIBRARY OF CONGRESS CATALOG CARD NUMBER: 72–11355

Contents

Preface

It seemed fairly clear in 1965 that large numbers of poorest black people were not going to share in the great victories being scored by the civil rights movement. There were plenty of reasons. The poorest black people had been steadily left out of the socio-educational process in which they might have been educated and motivated to participate in the regular American experience. They remained largely unacquainted with the world of machines, time schedules, and (white) social conventions. Furthermore, they tended to have criminal records. In a lot of cases the records were bad. So they weren't going to make it. The very civil rights controversies going on around them were about them, really, since their plight was being used to assault the conscience of the nation, but going on *around* them and leaving them out of the final settlements.

These poorest black people were a weirdly preconstitutional question. No one had just cynically decided to rule them out of the republic. But somehow they were out of the republic, whether considering their non-civil-rights or the horizon of their nonopportunity. That was the rub. The Constitution considers them citizens like everyone else born in America. But they seemed to be locked out of the chance to utilize their (purely abstract) rights. If one can imagine it, they were living a question which they put in words like these: "Are you all gonna keep us outa the country we was born in?"

Since 1965 that question has lost none of its urgency, but it has undergone some changes in registration and understanding. The vague "you-all" addressed in the question have acquiesced in the matter of allowing their official representatives to prepare several different answers to the question, each of them progressively tougher. By 1971 the people raising the question had been clapped into jail. One knows, particularly after the disturbing news issuing from jail (Attica, Joliet, Folsom, San Quentin, Soledad, Pontiac, etc.), that the people raising the question are not satisfied with jail as an adequate answer to their question.

I have written a brief memoir on what happened to that question on the south side of Chicago during the years 1965–71. It is a memoir in the sense that it is what I remember. The book is not about me. I was pastor of the First Presbyterian Church during the period. I enter the history only as a bearer of the question. The Blackstone Rangers likewise enter the history as they bear, utter, and *are* the question. The book is not about the First Presbyterian Church, except as it is related to the question. The subject of the memoir is strictly a question, no more than that. The stories of the Blackstone Rangers and the First Presbyterian Church are interesting in their own right and should be told. To tell them now would tempt understanding onto a colossal detour away from the question. The memoir is concerned with the manner of the question, the way it comes up, and seeks to present crucial historical events from the side of the lower-than-poor. It is, hence, largely narrative. Description of crucial events has been undertaken in order to provide focus to the question. The book is about a question, first of all: "Are you-all gonna keep us outa the country we was born in?" If it seems a little abrasive in that direct head-on form, the question could be stated more formally.

Shall every person born within the United States of America be considered an American, be accorded his constitutional rights and all derived social and economic felicities; or, shall an unspecified vast majority of persons enjoy those rights and annex to themselves the further right to exclude whom they select from full rights and derived felicities, without those procedures of selection being specified or subject to constitutional review?

It is a fully unpopular question, in fact, an absolutely rotten question. Who wants to deal with *that* at this late date? No one. Because it is so confounding, or has been switched around into another form —a question of violence, and public safety, and black revolution, and such—and with a sigh of relief passed over to the law-enforcement agency, the question has not been got up there into a really permanent and serious indismissibility. But what could this mean, with 1976 practically upon us? One has to suppose that the celebration of glorious revolution, all those pageants, the re-signing of the Declaration of Independence, the reratification of the Constitution will be going on safely, plump virtues protected from possible skewering by maniac black power because it is all in jail. The eyes glaze. Boggle goes the mind.

More immediately, we have survived another national election. Neither party had an exactly distinguished record of dealing with *any* vexing problems before the election. Those records were not sullied by attention to this great question. Far from being raised into serious and permanent indismissibility, it wasn't even raised. But one must realize the reason why it could have been ignored. The very people with demonstrated abilities to raise it are in jail, in hiding, in a narcotic stupor, or in exile. So who was there to laugh out loud when the citizens virtuously got themselves up and pledged allegiance to "One nation under God . . . with liberty and justice for all [but maniac black power] . . ."?

Difficult as eventual political solutions of problems represented by the question will be, the raising of the question is the more difficult. That is not a political matter. The political matter comes later as political attention focuses on the problems. But the precondition for getting the problems on the national agenda is finding the question relentlessly serious. And that is not going to happen with the question languishing in unpopularity and its raisers in jail. It is much too late in the game, voters too smart, to imagine some new orgy of violence if "something isn't done." That violence need not be promised, it is going on inside prison walls already. The question would be obscured were the officials of government to construct a battery of programs to forestall violence. No, that won't do.

It is backwards. The citizens of the republic will have to acknowledge the astonishing—and illegal—violence done to these poorest of all in the name of constitutional democracy. Moreover, the citizens of the republic will have to grant the great question its rightful place as the indismissibly dominant question facing the nation. ("And no jive.") Handling it will probably be easier than facing it.

Part One

The Defiant Lower-than-Poor

Ordinary analysis makes no provision for the lower-than-poor, lumping poor and lower-than-poor together in the sloppy category "black poor." The lower-than-poor know there is a great difference. They suffer more than the regular black poor and they are defiant, too. They resist the authorities—"give 'em fits." As though in prison they struggle against their guards. They are alien-natives whose resistance spooks regular Americans and their police.

1　Resistance Meets Pride

A young Stone, no more than eleven years old—a "Junebug"—
walked west on 47th Street near Ellis Avenue, Chicago, one afternoon
after school. It was March, 1969. He wore old pants, a thin jacket,
sneakers, no socks, and a brilliant red felt beret. He would not call it
a red beret or even a hat. It was a "sun." He would insist it be called
a sun. It announced he was not an ordinary ghetto kid; he was a
member of the Black P. Stone Nation. He might have been picking
up some groceries for his mother, or going to hang for a while with
the brothers at the candy store. He probably wouldn't get his business
done, whatever it was. That sun on his head was a sure ticket to a
hassle and perhaps a trip to the Prairie Avenue Police Station.

A blue-and-white squad car of the Chicago Police Department was
cruising eastbound on 47th Street. The patrolmen in the car spotted
the Stone on the other side of the street. They slowed down, both
looking at him, then made an abrupt U-turn. Headed west, they
moved up slowly alongside the boy. The patrolman nearest him rolled
down the car window and said something. The Stone did not look
toward the car or stop walking. That obviously wouldn't do. The
policemen stopped the car and got out, putting their hats on as they
walked up behind him. Policeman number one reached him first,
grabbed his shoulder roughly, and spun him around to face them.

I couldn't hear what they were saying. I was on the other side of the street in my car. I had seen the incident arising and thought the kid might need some eyewitness, so had stopped to watch. Clearly the police were saying something to the boy; as clearly, the boy was not responding. He stood there waiting to turn around and continue on to wherever he was going. After a minute or so of this one-way conversation the first policeman suddenly grabbed the sun and threw it down onto the sidewalk, covered as it was with March slush and mud. Then he stepped on the sun and smeared it around in the goop. Satisfied, he looked up at the Stone. He was looking at his sun. He bent down and picked it up and put it on his head at about the same rakish angle. The slush began to run down the sides of his head and onto his face as he turned and continued westward.

The two policemen stared at the boy walking away from them. They looked at each other. Firmer steps seemed called for. They went after the boy. Policeman number two this time reached the boy first and grabbed him around the neck with both hands. He was shaking the Stone *and* choking him. There was a kind of exasperation in the effort. "Why won't this kid break?" When the patrolman had finished, the boy half stumbled out of the grasp but didn't fall—or massage his necks muscles. Both policemen walked around in front of the boy. Policeman number two pointed back down the sidewalk where the confrontation had begun. The boy didn't look back. He still had not spoken a word to them. The second policeman took the muddy sun and smashed the thing right into the gutter, where, added to the sidewalk goop was broken glass, a lot more water, plus the usual stuff which makes Chicago gutters so much resemble sewers, such as candy-bar wrappers, dead rats, beer cans, orange peels, used Kotex, doll arms, bottle caps, shit, half burned telephone books, cigarette butts, and the like. The gesture was the kind you have seen Oliver Hardy make. It said, "What are you going to do about *that,* you dumb kid?" Clearly agitated, the policeman stepped on the sun, and almost as an afterthought, tromped it through some broken glass to the bottom of the gutter.

The Stone watched. When he believed the policeman had finished, he stepped away from them, squatted beside the gutter and felt around for his sun. As he lifted it out, it dripped with muddy water. It had been torn by the broken glass. Instead of emptying it onto the sidewalk, he placed it on his head again, this time giving no attention to a cool angle. The slime oozed down. He made no move to wipe it away. He said nothing. He looked straight ahead as he wheeled and began walking away. The policemen watched him go. A few moments later they returned to the car and after making a wide U-turn, continued cruising eastbound.

The "mighty men of Blackstone," some of them only eleven years old, say: "Let the mothers come on. Do their meanest shit. Blackstone win every time."

The policemen had just passed by dozens of boys the same age, dressed in the same ghetto uniform, and had not stopped. The ghetto lay before their eyes in a March-gray lassitude. The touch of red in the landscape had had a galvanizing effect on them. The ghetto suddenly arose from its passivity and asserted defiance. The sun was like a volley of sniper shots. The policemen believed a sun *had* to be a direct insult to their authority. No matter that the wearer is only eleven years old—perhaps younger—he is a Stone; so he will always resist the authorities.

The Stone agrees with that, except he adds something of his own to qualify "authorities." The authorities he is set up to resist are "the polices" who "do mean shit," who are, furthermore, "mothers" = motherfuckers = men who abuse defenseless ghetto women—*his* mother included—without fear of punishment and unconstrained by notions of human equality or dignity. The authorities appear as evil agents of a great power located down in the Loop somewhere. They jump out at you and seize you. They seek to frighten you. They want to rob you of something important by making you turn your eyes downward in fear. But they must not succeed. They must be resisted at all costs.

The young Stone feels himself a target of these authorities. He is an alien on 47th Street although he was born and raised in that immediate area. The other boys, exactly like him in age, dress, and demeanor, are the regular poor, occupying space in the conventional ghetto; the police drive past them having seen and seen through them into the unremarkable passivity. But the Stone is remarkable. His sun marks him an alien, eligible for confrontation with the authorities as surely as if he were wearing a yellow Star of David on the streets of an occupied European city in March, 1940.

But he is no passive alien. His calm before the policemen is belligerent. He refuses to admit their authority. He ignores their lethal weapons, preferring gladly the gutter slime on his head and neck to their obscene hands. Mr. Super-Cool, at eleven years old, forces the confrontation to its dizzy limits. "I'll wear the sun till you kill me. If you dare." A premonition of his defiance beguiled the policemen into the confrontation. Of course he must be beaten back into passivity. What else? The anomalous touch of red among the slanting grays and mud browns must be destroyed.

It was not destroyed that afternoon any more than it had been destroyed in hundreds of similar confrontations which went before. The bravura "Blackstone win every time" deserves more careful attention than thundering cries of civil libertarians on seeing two armed and dangerous men accost a little boy without reason or provocation. What is going on here?

I call it "psychological shoot-out."

Late in the summer of 1966 a squad car was parked in front of the First Presbyterian Church of Chicago in anticipation of a meeting of the Blackstone Rangers. One of the policemen in the car recognized Jeff Fort walking by and called him over to the car. Jeff Fort is one of the two "chiefs" of the Ranger organization.

"Gonna have another fifty guys and call 'em five hundred?" he asked, referring to recently published accounts of the size of Ranger meetings.

Jeff laughed. "That's right," he said, leaving the policeman in the firm belief that Jeff believed he was a pretty good wit.

During the meeting Jeff made an announcement to the fellas.

"Our president been sayin' we's fat. We's lazy. We's outa shape. Our president wants strong American boys. So we goin' for a walk."

The announcement was greeted with considerable enthusiasm, applause, and shouts of "Black . . . STONE!" A lesser leader followed Jeff to the pulpit of the church and explained the mechanics of the physical fitness march. They would walk out of the front door of the church single file, ten yards between each Ranger. They would walk east on 64th Street, across Stony Island Avenue—five blocks away—through Jackson park, back across Stony Island, west on 67th Street, then north on Kimbark Avenue to the church.

Jeff was going to show his fifty fellas to the wit in the squad car. There happened to be well over a thousand Rangers at the meeting that evening. He would see fifty fellas all right. In the same way Jeff hadn't acknowledged that Lyndon Johnson was yet president or that Jack Kennedy was dead, he didn't acknowledge the presence of traffic on Stony Island. This is a major four-lane north-south thoroughfare. It carries a full load of traffic at the end of the day. And there is no traffic light at the intersection. But if our president wants physical fitness, then out into the traffic the Rangers are going to go. And they did. They barged out into that mass of trucks, buses, and cars. The traffic had to stop. Once stopped, it couldn't start again, because the line of Rangers kept coming on and on and on and on. In fact, half the Rangers were not yet out of the church when the head of the march was already into Jackson park. And when the head of the march re-entered Stony Island three blocks south it halted the 67th Street traffic. So there was a memorable traffic jam, the policemen realizing that attempts to halt the march would prolong it. They endured to the end.

"Gonna have another fifty guys and call 'em five hundred?"

"Let the traffic back up to Gary, mother. You's lookin' at Blackstone Rangers."

In psychological shoot-out opponents dare each other to use lethal force, but in such a way that the user loses. It is a most righteous scene. Anything up to lethal force exists as a shill—a bluff. Strong nerves are required to overcome the bluff and win.

Some psychological shoot-out was played, incidentally, during the famous raid on First Church in the fall of 1966 (See Appendix for a detailed account of the events which led up to the raid, and a description of the raid itself.) There were a hundred or so Rangers in the building when the raid began. They were playing ball, dancing, just hanging, and some Ranger leaders were having a conference with city housing officials in the pastor's study. The police immediately seized all the Rangers and lined them up, hands high on the walls of the first- and second-floor hallways. They were thoroughly searched. Nothing was found. They were moved carefully up to the third-floor gym and made to stand around the walls, facing outward. Policemen with shotguns cradled in their arms lectured them on how dead they were going to be if they didn't get out of the Blackstone Rangers. One of the policemen made sure he accidentally hit a Ranger in the jaw with the barrel of his shotgun. Other policemen walked around the room, showing the Rangers that the safeties on their weapons were off. Another policeman saw a basketball on the floor and took a shot. He made it. The ball came out of the hoop onto the head of a Ranger directly underneath, standing just there and nowhere else by explicit order of the police. All the policemen laughed. Not so much as one facial muscle in one Ranger face twitched.

None of them moved for ninety minutes, in fact. They could hear the destruction going on in the next rooms, and the laughter accompanying the destruction. Their newly acquired (ancient) TV set, their pool table, their Ping-Pong table were being wrecked. They were to understand by that, apparently, that they were not supposed to have such great leftover stuff white folks were finished with. But through it all, they didn't move. They did, however, stare at the guards with undisguised contempt.

Eventually a sergeant came up and told the guard detail on the third floor that the raid was over. They all went down the stairs. One hundred Rangers suddenly found one word in their mouths without being signaled, without any white-boy "one, two, three," either. The guards which had gone to such great lengths to inspire fear may have been the least bit fearful themselves on hearing an ear-shattering "Black . . . STONE!" ricocheting off the walls of the church.

"When a hassle come up, it's jest gonna be who's got the most balls.

And which one got most gonna win." This Stone wisdom explains a lot. Consider the next report.

A very little boy, who couldn't have been more than three years old, was playing on the sidewalk in front of an apartment on Kenwood Avenue one very hot summer day in 1969. Maybe it was his daddy sitting on the steps of the building, drinking beer and watching the child play. He was a Stone, anyway. He had been back from Vietnam for only a few days. Some older kids came up and wangled the valve on a fire hydrant in front of the building so that they could have a romp in the water. The little boy was ecstatic. He joined right in, yelling and splashing around as though he were just a great big boy. The Stone appreciated the fun.

A young white policeman drove by. He hesitated. But he had after all seen a clear violation of the law, and he did have his duty to do, no matter how distasteful. He turned the water off and ran everybody out of the water. The older kids ran away cursing the policeman. But the little boy didn't run anywhere because he was where he was supposed to be. Probably he didn't want to get out of the water. So the policeman told the child directly to get out of the water. No response. He started to move after the child.

"Don't mess with the kid," the Stone said.

The policeman paused, then started after the child again. But he didn't make it. The Stone was off the steps in a blur. In a single motion he chopped the policeman's neck, took his revolver out of its holster, grabbed his left arm, twisted, and there he was, face down in the dirt, stunned, disarmed, and at the mercy of the Stone.

"I *said,* don't mess with the kid." With that the Stone threw the revolver down beside the policeman and went back up the steps for another drag on his beer.

The stakes in this shoot-out were higher, but the issue was the same. An officer had been assaulted. He had technical reason to pick up his revolver and shoot the Stone, or arrest him, or call for help. Except, how could he do any of those things? What story could he invent to cover the obvious facts that a single unarmed man had disarmed him, then given his gun back? Were he to shoot the maniac, the policeman would lose everything. Of course he could cut a notch in his gun. But life is not the issue in psychological shoot-out. Manhood is. And if he were to shoot, he would lose everything. He would know, the Stone would know, the boys up the street would know, the neighbors would know that the gun he might use in the shooting had been taken away *and* returned. He lost. And he didn't shoot the Stone. He did a manly thing and backed down. He picked up his revolver, put his hat on, got in his car, and let the kids come back to play in the water.

What does one make of these stories? An old man I knew went wild when he heard them. He was sick and seldom got out of his house. Sometimes I went to see him. The first thing he wanted to know was what the Rangers were up to. He couldn't contain himself when he heard. It was almost too much for him, yet he wanted the stories repeated again and again.

"When we were kids coming up," he said, "it was different. We didn't give the man any sass. He had that gun, you know. He'd hit you with it, too. That was that. Yassa, you was sure nuff sorry for anything he said you did, even if you never heard of it until right then. You was ready to let him know sure as hell who was boss. *He* was. We hated him much as these kids do but we were nice. We took it. We smiled. But these kids nowadays. . . ." His voice trailed off in wondering admiration. He was in a fantasy, recomposing his childhood. There he was standing up to the man, acting real cute, so quiet and cool, giving the man hell. I could tell his mind was fifty years away, back in Mobile or St. Louis. He was living it the way it should have been. He was *winning*.

That's the name of the game. If the authorities are going to play psychological shoot-out, by God, play their game and win. That is one of the things so impressive about the Stones. They invert the conventional ghetto confrontation between policeman and people.

Passivity is the convention in the ordinary confrontation. The policeman has the gun. It gives him the right to arrest you, then lie about you in court, and thus make you spend the next five years in jail. Ordinarily you do not give him any trouble. It might do your soul some good to fight him, but it does your soul no good to be dead. He is a threat because he is. He is a threat because he has a gun and is licensed to use it. He knows you know that. He has a big headstart on you before a confrontation arises. Why, he can do practically anything he wants and you don't dare cross him. He can get instant respect, a free screw, a witness, money, a drink, dope, and, always, evidence of your certain fear. You don't dare resist him. If you do, well . . . think about it.

That is the conventional scene. That is what is happening normally. The policeman has it all his way. The old man said it. "You was ready to let him know sure as hell who was boss. *He* was." But what advantage does he have, *really?* Suppose you do resist him, then what? Will he actually go for his gun? Will he arrest you? Merely to have asked the question is to have broken the man's principal advantage, which is, your unswerving belief in the certainty he will mess you up. Your belief swerves when you ask that question. You don't know what he will do. And he doesn't either. Defiance has the effect of erasing *his* greatest advantage, which is a belief in your unswerving belief.

The man throws his weight around. He roughs you up. He threatens you. But you don't knuckle under and smile. Now what? Will he hit you with a blackjack or the butt end of his revolver? Will he call you some obscene racist name? Or will he threaten you directly with a terrible vengeance? Suppose he does mess you up worse. He had to do it in order to get the respect you have withheld, so if he doesn't get the respect after doing that, he is in a deeper hole than when he started. It is a risk for him. He is in the minus numbers already, humanly speaking, by trying to win respect for his authority by misusing it. The more he misuses it, the more reason he gives you not to acknowledge his authority. If he becomes angry in the face of your calm, he takes a big risk in expressing his anger. You just might become calmer. In that case, he has lost heavily. In fact, once defiance has entered the conventional confrontation, he has lost. You have dared him to go ahead and do it, pull that gun out of its holster.

Now, of course, you do not obviously dare him. You do not fall into his way of human relations, which is a way of ridicule, curse, and threat. You dare him to use the gun by sinking into an absolute deep-freeze. You do not acknowledge he exists, much less that you are frightened of him. Not a flicker of the eye; not a twitch of a muscle. In that way you withhold respect and dare him to do something about it. "Let the mothers do their meanest shit, Blackstone win every time." Being translated, this means, "You not my boss. You not gonna be my boss by doin' bad. Never."

There it all is. The conventional scene has been turned upside down. Perhaps it doesn't sound like much but it spells the end of ghetto passivity and automatic fear of the unquestioned activities of the authorities. Heaven has not ordained that the police will win at psychological shoot-out. Once the people see two can play, there is a chance to win. That Blackstone will win *every* time may sound excessive. Mark it up to youthful arrogance. It must be admitted, however, that resistance is a heady experience. To beat the man at his own game sets the racial blood on fire. Malcolm X should have lived long enough to see it. He would have known. "Win, Jack, mess up the dude's mind; that's the thing."

It is not transparently clear that resistance to the authorities is what is going on as Rangers and police confront each other. In fact, the Ranger reputation obscures the possibility that it could be going on. One picks up the newspaper and reads of another dead kid. Rangers are said to be suspected of the murder. The stomach turns. One hears barroom gossip about this or that caper the Rangers pulled. School kids tell of having to give their money to the Rangers. Other school kids tell of being beaten because they would not join the Rangers. Ther is a constant murmur throughout the south side of Chicago about Ranger-related murder, robbery, rape, extortion, and terror. One has heard so much for so many years. The reputation has avalanched into a confusion of facts, rumors, and lies. Who can tell any more what the Rangers have done and what is blamed on them? With such a reputation, who cares to observe the difference? The Rangers surely have done something in order to have all of that terrible stuff blamed on them. The ordinary citizen laughs bitterly when he hears that the Rangers are resisting the authorities. "What is this *psychological* shoot-out crap?" he asks. "Why not *real* shoot-out? The cops should shoot the bastards dead, every one of them."

The Stones have little concern for what the precious ordinary citizen thinks, or the police. They are both the same anyway. That is what the Stones are resisting: the whole rotten uncomprehending pussheaded bunch of ordinary citizens with their guns, hard eyes, lead souls, and *their* cops. The time for transparent clarity has arrived. The Black P. Stone Nation *is* resistance, *is* over 3,000 black young men saying a giant hell-no to America. It could be they are the first wave of a new generation of ghetto young people or the last wave of the old. But they are trouble either way, since they are untouched by America's choice few million words of condemnation. That is what they resist. Realism advises the ordinary citizen to shut up. He has been listened to enough. Realism recommends, if curiosity has not already leaped ahead, some careful attention to an organization of such endurance and wrath.

In the interests of such realism the following brief description of Blackstone is offered, by no means conclusive or definitive: a starting place for vigorous thought rather than a pretended last word.

"Blackstone" is a nickname, a shortened form of the "Black P. Stone Nation," whose members are called "Stones." "Blackstone" is also the term used to stand for "Blackstone Rangers," and that was the previous name of the organization. Long before the young men who came to be known as "Stones" had the idea of a "nation," they were "Blackstone Rangers." They named themselves that because they were living around Blackstone Avenue in Woodlawn, and "Ranger" was the last name of "Lone." "Ranger" was not any more or less rich in vibrations than names other kids in the immediate vicinity were calling themselves. "Rangers" could have well been Comanches, Maniacs, Falcons, Pimps, Casanovas, Aces, FBI's, Kings, or Apaches. But these particular kids around Blackstone Avenue chose "Rangers."

There were between ten and twenty kids in the first batch of Rangers. They were aged twelve to fifteen. As they began to band together, kids just like them were organizing on their south, north, and west. (Lake Michigan lay to the east.) Had the Rangers followed the Chicago script, they would have grabbed up ugly weapons and headed south for a war with the organization there. But the Rangers turned out to be different. They had been coming out of reform school and they had a new angle. More like case-hardened cons than mere little boys, the Rangers moved south for a parlay. "You join us," they said," and the two of us can move on the Harper Boys (to the immediate north of both groups)." It worked. The Rangers talked themselves past a war into an agreement. Since they had thought of the scheme, the Rangers had the lead. The two groups, coming as one group—but, in truth, two groups held together by the flimsiness of a mere agreement—walked north to Harper. The Harper Boys couldn't tell that there were two groups. They saw total fellas in front of them in clearly superior numbers. So the ordinarily ferocious Harper Boys found themselves compelled to talk. The three groups talked about their number one worry to the west: the Disciples. The area has got to be protected against the Disciples. The Harper Boys were enthusiastic about that. Well, "Why not the three of us be one of us?" Each club would continue to have its own organization, of course, its own officers, and its own meetings, but all three would be together and would also be Blackstone Rangers as well as whatever else they were, such as Maniacs and Harper Boys.

The original three-in-one organization was located in the southeast quadrant of Woodlawn. The members were not content to stay there only. A plan was developed. They decided to fight the "D's" whenever they had to or wanted to. They decided also to begin recruiting new fellas into the existing clubs and to begin organizing brand-new clubs in the northeast quadrant of Woodlawn. There hadn't been any permanent clubs yet in that area. Of course, twelve- and thirteen-year-old kids organize into all kinds of clubs about twice a week. Nothing had caught hold and lasted, however. The Ranger confederation came north and formed clubs which did take hold and last. The local kids were not stupid. They had heard about the Rangers as soon as there were Rangers to be heard about. They had been figuring on what the Rangers meant. So when Rangers came up their back steps and began talking friendly like, well, it was a positive relief and joy. You bet they wanted to get something started. They would be pleased to name themselves something that ended with Rangers. No sooner said than done.

To understand what was happening in these early days, one does well to cosider that a twenty-five-member club is big and if it stays together longer than a year it is old. The Blackstone Rangers started with more than fifty members. According to the Chicago script, these Woodlawn guys should have been breaking up, fighting among themselves, and regrouping a year later, or at about the time they actually were close to doubling their original size. They were unique even then. Something about the way they talked around *and* fought the (goddamned) D's showed class. They had style. They were definitely admirable. They knew how to do the main business, and young fellas just had to be attracted to them.

The recruiting and organizing of new clubs was a spectacular success. Stone memories of those early membership totals confuse myth with reality and are not trustworthy. To believe Stones, one would conclude there were more than 250 Rangers in 1963, and 500 in 1965. The actual numbers are not of great consequence. The rapidly growing Ranger confederation was of sufficient size to promise hell to all potential members without having to make the threat. That is the point. Rangers drifted over into the living area to the south and east of Woodlawn, for instance. This is the South Shore neighborhood. There was a club there which called itself the "Golden Falcons." The presence of Ranger emissaries come in peace for the purpose of talking served to emphasize the smallness of the single Falcon club compared to the mighty Ranger confederation, which could get away with sending emissaries! The Falcons joined up instantly. Old-time Falcons have told me that the threat played no part in their decision to join the Rangers. They liked the Ranger style. The wanted to join, and had been hoping they would be asked.

I was not in Woodlawn during the first five years of the Blackstone history. I am reporting what I have heard from a variety of Stone and non-Stone sources. Even after allowing for a normal inflation of numbers which imagination more than memory suggests, it is nevertheless clear that the numbers of fellas in the Ranger confederation were unprecedented on the south side, and perhaps in Chicago. And the stories of how the confederating worked seem to be trustworthy. They conform to what I saw after I came to Woodlawn.

The Ranger style could not have been successful without the unfailing cooperation of a system of heartless authorities. The Rangers did not force people to knuckle under. They came by kids just like themselves who were being *always* forced to knuckle under and were despising it. When the Rangers came by they offered a different way. "You don't hafta git on your knees. Don't hafta take that shit." The very idea of not taking it sets up resonances within the core of any ghetto kid who has ever lived. There would be no Ranger reputation or Ranger organization unless the Rangers had this absolutely evangelical idea concerning resistance. The idea had a group of potential believers virtually as wide as the ghetto youth population. They didn't have to knuckle under.

Organizing style *was* the Ranger style. In dealing with new fellas or new clubs, the Rangers did not force the issue, the way police, teachers, or momma would do it, so that after being forced, the new fellas would hate their conquerors. It is unproductive for an organizer to force membership; the organizer knows too keenly the humiliation of being forced. The confederating style respects the very human desire not to be run over. During the early months of my association with Blackstone, the Rangers were in the period of their biggest expansion. They were confederating with clubs as far north as 31st Street and as far south as 95th Street. When they brought new club members to the church, the visitors were accorded dignity and the considerations due visiting heads of state. The Rangers were not feigning respect—jiving. The visitors' accomplishments were substantial. A leader is a leader, cherished by Blackstone because of demonstrated talents.

These various clubs should have been fighting each other into the ground, until, exhausted and drained of resources, they would stagger off into adulthood, the better to boast the remainder of their days about when *they* were gang-bangers. But these Ranger clubs were not fighting each other. They were pooling strength peacefully. They were achieving an organization of unprecedented size. Nothing in the Chicago history of poor black boys resembled the Ranger system. Between April, 1966, and the end of the year, the organization grew from 500 to 1,500 members. During the twelve months of 1967 the number doubled. The power of the organization was well known to south side residents and the police, but not nearly as well known as to the members themselves. Every one of them had had some hand in creating their organization. The Ranger leaders might very well be spectacular guys, but the essence of Blackstone lies in the membership, each one of which has the personal belief he has barged into something brand new and enormously exciting. To be a Ranger was to be really black for the first time. Really black people do not take it. That's what Negroes do. Black people resist. This is an apocalyptic idea when it occurs inside the head of a fourteen-year-old boy as a result of doing it, not reading it or hearing it. Three thousand black people all together make the task of each one of them 3,000 times easier. Each Ranger had to make up his own mind about resistance. He had to come to terms with his long-standing fear of the authorities. He had to face that time when he would be alone, the entire weight of black history concentrated in his being, and then be assualted by the authorities. Would he vindicate the honor of his people? Would he bear up under the strain of confrontation? He had to make that personal decision inside himself before it happened. It was a task made 3,000 times easier because 2,999 others had had to face the same thing.

The critical event in the history of Blackstone occurred on December 28, 1966. On that night resistance was transmuted into affirmation and a nation was born.

Earlier that day members of First Church's staff invited the two Ranger chiefs, Jeff Fort and Eugene Hairston, to lunch following a long meeting. All were walking to a nearby restaurant when a young man passed who said his ritual "Black . . . STONE!" to the chiefs.

Neither Jeff nor Gene knew him and he seemed to be a Ranger. They both laughed uneasily. They were a brotherhood grown so big the leaders didn't know the members. A chill fell on the lighthearted group strolling over for lunch. The chill was a simultaneous recognition inside six consciousnesses that he could be a police informer. No one spoke of the freshly awakened dread or of anything else until after the group had arrived at the restaurant and ordered. Then Jeff and Gene began to confess appalling secrets to each other. Both of them had had similar experiences repeatedly in the previous weeks and had been holding back on the other out of sheer vanity.

The danger of potential informers didn't have to be talked about since everyone at the table knew its scope. The danger would not be comprised in the truth an informer might tell, but the lies he *would* tell under the cloak of actual membership. The group realized an extreme vulnerability which had to be repaired immediately. The director of First Church's Ranger Staff, Chuck Lapaglia, recommended that the problem be considered as a mere problem in size and not a problem in Blackstone loyalty. "If you guys know everybody, or even if you make sure the leaders altogether know everybody," he said, "you have the problem of informers licked. Your problem is that you are too good at your jobs. You are too successful." Seen as an organizational problem, the chiefs could put their heads together and come up with something. Before lunch was finished they had a new organizational set-up ready to be put into effect. It would provide for the informer problem and might even make a stronger organization. Generally the proposed set-up called for Gene to be the chief of all the older fellas. They would be called Blackstone Rangers. Jeff would be the chief of the younger fellas and they would be called "Black Princes." It was a sign of their mutual understandings that no hard line was drawn between older and younger fellas. Presumably it would just happen naturally. The staff could tell that the chiefs felt they had made an inspired decision. Chuck asked when this reorganization was going to take place. The chiefs were incredulous that he should even ask. "Tonight." Of course.

The meeting that night was semi-select. Not all the clubs had been

invited, surely not the newest clubs. Some doubtful clubs, on probation, wouldn't have been invited as a matter of policy. Only the trusted
and true men of Blackstone had been informed of the meeting—
ironically called because some of them, or even *one* of them, might
not be completely trustworthy or true. At any rate, there were lots of
people on hand. The full-sized gym was solid fellas. For effect the
overhead lights had been changed from the usual glaring white 300-
watt lights for playing basketball under to a soft combination of
forty-watt green, blue, and red lights. The effect was sensational-eerie-
important. About ten o'clock Gene and Jeff appeared on the balcony
to one side of the gym, upon which rich white parents had once stood,
fondly watching their sons play.

Gene spoke first. He took Chuck's line about being too successful
and put some black English on it.

"We's got too big for our britches," he said. "Hear me now. Got
too mean. Yah. Gonna hafta see bout them Rangers. What all them
cats think they doin'? They beginnin' to think they really is somebody.
Jest *loook* at 'em prancin' round yellin' at the good niggers. Gonna
hafta see bout them Rangers. Yah. Got way too big for their britches
. . ." and so on. He didn't have to mention the problem of possible
Ranger perfidy because he was purposefully turning the organization
around in the assumed gaze of the authorities. He didn't have to say,
in just plain words, "If you were the police, and you hated Rangers,
what would you do?" He was saying the same thing in the mode of
humor and good fun. So he carried the point of his great announcement on the back of necessity; no one could accuse him or Jeff of
breaking up the good old ways. He insisted nothing was going to
change except to get better.

Jeff spoke next. He explained in pedestrian terms what was going
to happen that night, who was going where, who was going to be
named what, and who was going to be leader of what.

The lights, the closeness, the speeches helped the organization become aware of itself in a surprising new way. The speeches were
frequently punctuated with blood-curdling yells of "Black . . .
STONE!" After the speeches, there was a parting of the company. The

older guys stayed in the gym with Gene. The younger fellas went with Jeff into the women's parlor of the church. This is the kind of room you see as Margaret Rutherford's living room in British movies. Dainty old chairs and divans, bric-a-brac, bookcases, heavy old rugs, and lined drapes. Old, crowded, and musty, it was an unlikely room for the events about to happen in it. The light crew had rigged red, blue, and green lights in the fixtures on the walls. The overhead lights were not used. The younger fellas walked into an even darker room than the gym, full of the unaccountable shapes of chairs and couches, and things. Most of them had never been in the room before. It was weird. It was crowded beyond describing. It was so hot and close a fella felt ready to . . . but he didn't, because if he thought he was hot, wait until his blood started catching on fire, and if he couldn't breathe, he hadn't faced the further problem of a runaway heart. That was exactly what Jeff was about to do to every kid in the room.

He started talking so quietly it was not clear he was talking, and certainly not clear what he was talking about. He didn't raise his voice. A fella had to want to hear very badly and strain to hear. If he caught the drift, he had no further difficulty in wanting to hear. Jeff started talking about black people in Africa who owned the place. They were rich and fat and they had their own governments, and they had kings who ran the governments, and they had princes who were studying on how to run the governments when their daddies died. These princes were young kings because they would be kings some day.

But they didn't make it. They were whipped, and tied up, and shipped to Alabama to work like dogs. It isn't right for princes to work like dogs in Alabama when they should be back in their own hood studying on how to run the government. A good many of the young men had been steadily tuning out all adult talk at them from three years old onward, so if they had had the chance to hear this basic story before, they wouldn't have been listening. Many of them would not have had the occasion to hear it. It was a gripping story. Jeff went back and forth across the Atlantic any number of times, between Alabama—his all-purpose slave state—and Africa. He was getting low but clear responses of anger. The idea was bolting in on the fellas. They knew in general that they had been fouled off into a crazy house by being born, but they had no idea of their origins. The grandeur was built up, then each time smashed by the reality of working like dogs in Alabama. Then Jeff came into the modern age:

"We not be havin' a real place here; we not gonna run this here American govament. We's still dogs—the way they look. They not even let us starve to death. They gotta be messin' over us all the time we's only tryin' to starve to death. Whooeee! No way we gonna run this here govament. All the studyin' we do ain't gonna change one thing. So what we gonna do? We gonna have our own govament, the way our daddies did long time back. And what peoples git messed up by the polices and such is gonna be our peoples. They don't let us in their govament, we git our own. They not let us *in,* we be OUT. In some kinda super way. We be the *out* boys for the *out* peoples. Yah. We be *outasite* boys."

This was responded to with laughter, shouts, warwhoops, and unrestrained affirmation. He was describing Chicago. It was the same story here as in Alabama, wasn't it? Instead of studyin' on how to run the govament, they were running down alleys to get away from mean polices, having to spend all their time protecting themselves and the people from attack. "That ain't right, cause WE'S ALL PRINCES." Sheer pandemonium broke out at such audacious truth. The fellas were screaming with the clarity of recognition. We are all princes, Jeff said, without pretty robes, without rings on our fingers, and crowns on our heads. But that stuff doesn't make a prince. A prince is a prince because he has been born into a royal family, which no one can take away from him. "How can a prince be told?" Jeff asked. A prince is beautiful, he is strong, and he comes from kings.

Tell that to a raggedy-ass thirteen-year-old boy whose stomach is growling because he has not eaten in twenty-four hours; tell that to a boy whose family moved away last summer without telling him where so that he has been alone in the world, sleeping in abandoned cars, doorways, living off scraps he can find and steal; tell that to a boy who has never known an instant's reprieve from the deadly requirements of sheer survival. He will explode with the force of the revelation. He will be staggered. He will tremble with rage and excitement. He will know himself to be a new man. He *is* a Black Prince.

The idea was not well formed or fully formed. It was still skyrocketing around inside their heads. But they were onto something, no doubt about that. They had experienced whatever it was. The words to tell the experience would come. "We the *out* boys," they began to say. They had to laugh about how true the statement was. It sure did sum them up completely.

After the reorganization younger fellas began to celebrate their new identity by writing it on buildings. "Prince" is easily said but not as easily spelled. I imagine the population was bewildered at the new legends which were appearing on the buildings of Woodlawn in January, 1967: black pren, print, pirin, prints, pirins, and so on. The difficulty in spelling the word was minor compared to the difficulty in getting proper names to describe the new elements of the reorganization. The Princes were still very much Rangers, meaning what the organization used to be called, but not Rangers, meaning what the reorganization called Rangers. All the permutations were tried. I saw them on pieces of paper in my office, some young men trying to find a way to write it down. Three words: Blackstone, Prince, and Rangers. No combination of those words came out right or looked right. Then an unknown Prince solved the problem. He scrawled out "Black P. Stone Rangers" one night on the wall of the local A & P store. When the chiefs looked at that the next day their eyes were blinded with light. Their understanding jumped light-years ahead of where it had been a moment ago. Blackstone is not the name of a street. Blackstone is the name of a people, and it can be read backwards. Blackstone means Stone Black. Just think of that. Hard like stone. Didn't that fit their own understanding of themselves? Wasn't stone the essence of resistance? Why hadn't they thought of it before?

"Stones" were born through the fingers of a little kid who was so far away from spelling "Prince" he could only get through the "P". Once seen, there were no more Rangers and no more Princes. The whole reorganization would be known as what they had always been:

Stone Black. Of course, oldtimers will say the most flattering possible thing about a fellow Stone with the words, "That Stone a *Ranger,*" meaning he is cut out of old cloth, in the mold of heroes.

With inexorable force, the idea of Stone as a comprehensive name for resistance, and "P" as a comprehensive letter for the Princes who lead the resistance pushed the Stones into an elaboration of the situation of resistance, the points of which were established by Jeff Fort in December. Although the word "nation" had been used before in Chicago to describe certain jerry-built youth associations, and, of course, had been fundamentally used by native Americans, it did not present itself in either of those frames of reference to the Stones. "Nation" was an outgrowth of the idea of being alien and being alien together, as "the out boys," and as the protectors of an out people. Thus, when the Stones eventually put it all down as the Black P. Stone *Nation* they were referring to all of the people in Chicago who were kept out. The stones understood themselves to be the leaders of this Nation. Later in 1967, during a press conference dealing with a local controversy, a Stone spokesman was asked what the words "Black P. Stone Nation" meant. Here is what he replied:

We's a nation now, so that's what we callin' ourselves from now on. We usetabe kids runnin' round here but we're growed up now; we got ourselves ladies and kidsa our own. We got old mens and old ladies, little tiny kids, Junebugs, mens, fellas, fellas in college, fellas in Vietnam; we got clubs in Cleveland, Milwaukee, and Gary, and all round the country. We's a whole nation, you understand, and that's what you oughta call us. The Black P. Stone Nation.

A reporter asked him, "What does the 'P' stand for?" He dissimulated. He answered, "All the things 'P' stands for. You know. People. Peace. Power. Prosperity. All that kinda thing." He hadn't thought of it before. He had made some rapid intellectual calculations, obviously, and had decided the press wasn't able to handle "Prince."

In my understanding of Blackstone history, "Stones" is a code word for "Princes." It was developed by the energy released in the galvanizing moment when the young guys understood themselves to be black princes on the way to recovering their latent splendor. "Stones" could not have come into existence otherwise. The allegiance Stones have to their organization is composed to a significant degree of allegiance to themselves as individual young black men. They have come to the meaning of the stone in resistance, and they have found it in their essence—in what they were born to be.

An attempt to break down his allengiace to Blackstone is not, in a Stone's terms, a matter of getting him to quit a social club, a gang. He is being asked to renounce himself. And he is flatly not going to do that. He is not going to renounce his being as a prince in order to resume his being a nigger kid.

One has the interest, perhaps, to return to the March afternoon scene. It is possible to see the Stone's unbending calm before his tormentors as something more than an act of resistance. It was a surge into being. As the scene is rerun in psychological slow motion, the dominant motif refracted through the boy's steady intention to continue on, his refusal to admit a mutuality with the patrolmen, his defiant letting the gutter filfth run down the sides of his head is . . . PRIDE.

Feelings of black pride (and rage) would not have been unusual for black young people anywhere in the United States in the spring of 1969—or now, for that matter. The drive for black identity is neither new nor finished. It exists in virtually all black organizations, including conservative ones. The drive doesn't seem to be going very far or very fast in most of these organizations, however. Pride in identity is sought by itself, as an abstract isolated goal. Hence one is enthralled by the spectacle of a black leader standing before cheering multitudes. He parses out the magnificent words:

> I am. . .
> Somebody.
> I may be poor
> I may be in jail
> I may be hongry

I may be on welfare
But
I am
Somebody.

The audience responds by shouting each expression back to him.

Undoubtedly there are psychic victories won in these experiences. But even those victories are hollow and the great words eventually return to haunt the shouter if the black leader is not leading the newly proud black enthusiast to seek a restoration of identity. "Somebody" does not go along with the expected motions of servitude. "Somebody" does not grin and do a little soft shoe for the white folks. There is no real recovery of identity without refusal to the man demanding the servility. At the same time, there can be no refusal without that act being a restoration of the "somebody." This is the experience of Blackstone. Its melding of the two realities into a single organic whole of resistance-pride places it at the forefront of black organizations in (or, to hear Stones tell it, out of) this country. These young men have paid their dues. They have not knuckled under and *have* given the man fits. Under all the pressure possibly to apply on them, they have nonetheless refused to say the damning, "Yassa, Marsh Daley." Few other Chicago-based black people can honestly say as much—or, as proudly.

2 The St. Charles-Woodlawn Jail

In the first year of the association which developed between First Church and Blackstone, Chuck Lapaglia saw that the Blackstone Rangers were unlike any street gang he had come to know in over ten years of experience as a youth worker on Chicago streets; furthermore, they were unlike any gang he had heard about. I was a newcomer to Chicago, thus was unprepared to assess Blackstone against Chicago experience, but I had previously worked with street gangs—in East Harlem and the Amsterdam housing project in New York City—and was aware that Blackstone was unlike either of these gangs. With such backgrounds Chuck and I sought to decipher the enigmatic clues which led us to believe Blackstone was possibly a new—but definitely a different—kind of youth organization. We soon enough found what we were looking for: Blackstone more resembled a prisoners' organization than it did a gang or a community organization. Not much digging was required, since the evidence lay on Blackstone's surface in abundance; we, therefore, cannot claim a special trophy for intellectual competence. But we can claim a medal, at least, for intellectual perseverance in seeking to alert First Church, the police, and general public to the far-reaching consequences of our modest discovery. We have contended that a proper understanding of Blackstone must begin with a consideration of the reform school which went before the Woodlawn beginning. Recall that the brief description of

Blackstone in Chapter 1 contained this statement: "But the Rangers turned out to be different. They had been coming out of reform school and they had a new angle. More like case-hardened cons than mere little boys, the Rangers moved south for a parlay." Unless the meaning of that statement is excavated, the brief description is not merely incomplete, it is misleading. Blackstone (as an idea and as an organization) did not begin in Woodlawn. It began in St. Charles.

St. Charles is the Illinois youth correctional facility of the Illinois state penitentiary located at Joliet, Illinois. Hardcore, repeating-type, criminally prone Chicago kids are sent to St. Charles for rehabilitation. It is a reform school, plain and simple. And a reform school is a prison for kids with psychological chintz nailed over the bars. St. Charles is a prison in the major meaning of the word: the inmates cannot get out. It is a prison like any other prison. Incorrigible boys are placed there in forced detention. It is like the real prison at Joliet for adult incorrigibles, and, more to the point, it is like the prison Dostoevski described, James Jones described, Alexander Solzhenitsyn described, Victory Hugo described, Emile Zola described, and even like the prisons described by the kindly doctors Karl Menninger and Robert Lindner. St. Charles has what all prisons have: warfare—the prisoners versus a highly organized detention apparatus composed of the warden, guards, chaplain, psychologist, social worker, and gym teacher; the prisoners are organized, too, although the staff might dispute such a fact.

Most of the young men sent to St. Charles come right off Chicago streets. In 1957–60 some of them came from Woodlawn. They are the ones we are interested in. They were not Alabama boys recently moved to Chicago. These boys had been born and raised in Chicago. They were street-wise, tough, and experienced beyond their years in the means and ends of violence. They were, precisely, incorrigible. They had records of assault, unlawful use of weapons, theft, larceny, truancy, and disorderly conduct. They had been remanded to St. Charles in the hope they might be rehabilitated. Perhaps the detention would shake them up. Perhaps they would learn to want to learn a useful occupation. At any rate, they had to be reconditioned so that they might be suited to the multiple requirements of living legal and socially useful lives. All of which exists in the theory of rehabilitation; the actuality of rehabilitation is discipline. These mean kids must learn, before anything else, who is boss.

The original Blackstone Rangers, those still living, remember St. Charles vividly. It was their first time in jail. When testifying before a Special Investigating Committee of the Presbytery of Chicago in 1969, Jeff Fort recalled those days with particular pointedness. He could not easily have forgotten. Two of the staff at St. Charles had become officials of the Cook County Jail (which comes closer to being Jeff's legal residence than his own home). As Jeff had graduated from juvenile to adult prison, so had those first tormentors. Jeff recalls St. Charles as a fight from go. The staff decided these tough kids like Jeff Fort especially must be shown instantly they can't get away with a thing. They must become accustomed to a routine of absolute discipline. "The man tell you to move, you move. He tell you to stop, you stop. He tell you when to eat, when to sleep, when to shit, when to be quiet, when to work, when to go to school. He bang you when he feel like it. He is the MAN." The Woodlawn kids ran into that and they said, "Bullsheeeit."

That's the one thing they wouldn't take. They saw through it. A Stone recalls, "They wanted to bust us *in our heads.* They done busted us to the joint, you understand. Soon's we git there they try to bust us in our heads. Make us soft like they is. Scare us. Beat us up, you know, like we was slaves that gotta get use to doin' what the masters say. No goddamn way that gonna work, *never.*"

The prison has a sensible system of rewards and punishments. Its punishments bring pain. Its rewards bring the pleasure of an end to the pain. The system was designed for an individual prisoner. He must be helped to see his comparative weakness and the comparative strength of the system. Accordingly a prisoner would see the one guard who whacks him and would relate that guard, sensibly, to all of the guards and their whacking him. Well, "one" can't stand up to them all. "One" can also be put into solitary confinement, "one's" food rations reduced. "One" can be given onerous tasks. "One" has no appeal mechanisms. There are no umpires in jail. "One" is helped, thereby, to accept the authority of the system's strength; "one" shuns the punishments and seeks the rewards.

The prison system is designed to produce a docile series of unrelated prisoners. The staff does not want to spend all of its time *doing* discipline. It wants to threaten harsh disciplinary measures so they won't be needed. Tractible and sensible prisoners are certain to go along with the system. The authorities do not allow themselves to think of organized, *mass* resistance among the prisoners, the sole purpose of which is to overcome the system. Can a system imagine its own overthrow? Hardly. The system does not, therefore, plan for the possibility of individual prisoners, emboldened by their solidarity with other prisoners, to shun the rewards and treat the punishment with contempt.

A prisoner is supposed to dread solitary confinement, according to the disciplinary design. The guards become angry when a prisoner goes to "the hole" defiantly. Obviously the plan is not working. Thus when he comes out of his solitary confinement full of good cheer, and hasn't whined, or begged, or cursed, the guard gives him some angry knocks with the rubber hose to *force* the plan to work. When the prisoner laughs in his face, he had better admit the plan won't work. Something going on among the prisoners has aborted the main end of the system. The individual is not docile and unrelated. He has gone into the shell of a mass of prisoners. A prisoners' system has been devised to thwart the outcome of the prison's system.

Because the prisoners mass themselves in order to resist the prison's system, the prison must concentrate its full attention and energy on breaking the resistance which is going on before its very eyes, if only it could be seen. But this resistance can't be seen because *it* goes out of its way to be invisible. It is secret. The only people who know anything about it are the people in the resistance and they are organized for the precise purpose of resisting the prison's effort to find out what is going on. The only means available to the prison staff is what is in its system. The staff spends time and goes to great lengths to determine the most breakable single suspected rebel, then sets about

breaking him. It uses the promise of unusual punishment, the promise
of unusual in-jail benefits, and the promise of an unusual reduction
of sentence as an offering to the selected rebel in return for desired
information on the suspected rebellion. This is what the Stone was
referring to when he said, "[They try to] make us soft like they is."
He meant corrupt, lazy, and mean.

But the prisoners have thought about that a long time ago and have
steeled themselves ahead of time against the corruption it represents.
How? By assuring themselves of the integrity of each new member of
the organization and, then, by preparing every member in advance for
the unusual confrontations. They knew clearly that an organization
is as strong as its weakest member. The idea is to have no weak
members. If a guy is weak, give him reason to be strong, or, better,
leave him out of the organization.

It is a perpetual warfare. It is often bloody. It is always violent.
Existing against the authorities' best efforts to break it, a prisoners'
organization institutes terror against other prisoners. It forces them
to join or to be silent in the face of interrogation. It represents such
terror that a prisoner learns to face the hostility of the guards gladly
rather than the hostility of his fellow prisoners who will gang-rape
him or kill him for sure if he "tells." Even the nice boys who get into
St. Charles—almost by a mistake of the courts—know the score.
Although treated by staff and prisoners as noncombatants, they learn
quickly, nevertheless, what to stay out of and, if they see anything,
what to be quiet about. Terror is the violent threat prisoners can pose
among themselves to themselves in order to maintain the security of
their resistance.

How does it start?

It is always starting. It starts with the arrival of a new boy. He
watched the gates open before him; he walks through them. They are
closed. Then, "Thunk!" He has been struck from behind a staggering
blow on the head. He turns around to see a guard fondling a long
narrow canvas bag filled with sand, popping it repeatedly into his
hands. "You my baby now. All the time you here, you my baby. Ain't
gonna be *no*body see what I do. Ain't nobody cares. Jest don't give

me no jive . . ." The guard leaves the expression dangling there. He does not add, " . . . and we'll get along fine," for that conclusion admits a mutuality between them. There is no mutuality. The expression is a pronouncement, more like an ominous warning; it is not intended to counsel the boy and make his way easier. Its sole purpose is to frighten him.

Each new boy does one of two things. He lowers his eyes in fear, thus signaling deference to the guard; or he glares in anger, thus signaling resistance to the guard. Resistance is always starting because new boys always coming in recognize the confrontation just inside the prison gates as something they have long known about and have long despised. It has happened to them before. That's momma's system; that's the school system; that's the police's system. "They's all the same!" They beat, yell at, threaten, withhold—to get you to do what they want. And you just *naturally* are not going to do it because of the way they are trying to get you to do it. So when you get to St. Charles and they go after you in that old, well-known way, but meaner, and no other way appears magically as a reprieve from the demands, then you are a resistance cell of one. Imagine the new boy's relief when he soon enough discovers he is not alone in his resistance and imagine the alacrity with which he pools his resistance with the resistance already started.

The organization of prisoners is universal, except in those rare penal institutions which do not rule prisoner life with physical force.* There was an organization of sorts among the inmates at St. Charles before the Woodlawn boys started coming in. It never was the same after they got there. I am talking about Eugene Hairston, Jeff Fort, Junior, J.J., Droop, Edward Bey, Throop, Chicken, Charley Franklin, Bo-Peep, Lefty, Porgy, Slim, Brown, Bop, Dee-Baby, Gypsy, Hutch, Grill, and a lot of other guys now dead. They had known each other before they got to St. Charles. So when they arrived, they had a lot of common boyhood experience between them to add to the "Bullsheeeit" every one of them just naturally said once they got there.

*See Karl Menninger's *The Crime of Punishment* (New York: Viking Press, 1968), Chap. 9, "Have There Been No Improvements?"

"Not so much we *started* somethin', understand. Somethin' already there. We make it work. We give'em fits. *We* begin to run it, not them. We run it. Yah. Stone run it way back then." The guy telling me this ten years after it happened had a glint of hard-earned pleasure in his eyes. "Stone run it way back then" was the revealing part of the statement, because he had never thought of the experience in *Stone* terms before. It was ridiculous. There was no Stone then, yet maybe there was. Maybe there was always Stone. He used "Stone run it," however, as a current expression and directed it backward ten years as an explanation—to himself—of what then occurred. Numerous similar reminiscences indicate the same thing. "Stone run it," is a prison expression primarily. When it is used as a contemporary slogan on the streets of the south side of Chicago it sounds the least bit immodest, for, by their own reckoning, they don't run it. What they run is "the glass, the busted-up cars, the tin cans, the wine bottles." What are they claiming they run when they write "Stone run it" in huge expansive letters across the buildings in their hood? One thing. Resistance. They are running the resistance in that part of their world, all of which had its beginning in running the resistance going on in St. Charles.

Blackstone was born in St. Charles as the self-appointed guardians of a resistance already underway. It was born under the watchful eyes of guards, wardens, gym teachers, and rehabilitation staff, which was intently trying to find out what these kids are up to and *which ones they are.* They came to the psychologist. He tested them. They refused to cooperate. They entered into veritable conspiracies of creativity in order to provide him with no answers or with nonsense answers. One of those psychologists later reported to a Senate Investigating Sub-committee that he had given Jeff Fort I.Q. tests on three separate occasions and on none of them had he scored higher than fifty-eight. "You better believe it, head doctor."

The fellas would come to meals and the whole crowd would refuse to eat—for no reason. They, furthermore, would screw up the games they were supposed to play. And the classes they were forced to attend became endurance tests for the instructors. The social workers were treated like spies, and an uneasy warden was mercilessly conned. They fought among themselves with a fervor matched only by the fervor they mustered in fighting the guards. The rehabilitation was not taking. The kids were resisting with a style ominously new, for they were enjoying it. The blandishments of cop-out offers were nothing compared to the glee won on refusing them. Indeed, these particular kids were "givin' em fits." And the more they did it, the stronger they got. The stronger they got, the more unity they developed among their fellow prisoners. In case one has forgotten, the boys we are referring to were aged twelve through fifteen.

The mechanics of their organization were hidden. They are still hidden. No one yet knows how they do it. They understand each other. They communicate. The chain of command works. But it is all veiled in secrecy. This is the fabled "business," they are attending to, the nature of which is not revealed to friends, supporters, family, girl friends, or, naturally, the screws.

It was learned under the eyes of the guards. It has no doubt been expanded and refined since then but basically learned there, where the problem was, how to get information to lots of people while the guards it is being kept from are watching. Master that problem, and some system of secret communication has been devised. Some organization has been devised, I should say, because the communication is secondary to the organization.

The outlines of the organization were also set in St. Charles. There were two indisputable leaders. They were the smartest, not necessarily the toughest or the meanest of the fellas. The two leaders were just "a teeny bit higher than" the council of which they were a part, which later came to be known as "The Main Twenty-One." By "teeny bit," a Stone once explained, is meant the thickness of a matchbook cover as compared to the height of the table. "The chiefs is *this* high," adding the flattened out matchbook cover to the height of the table. He was trying to tell me that neither Gene nor Jeff were primarily big chiefs, they were first members of the council, which was the collective leader of the organization; they were two among many leaders. They had learned it all in St. Charles, where they had learned the necessity of having lots of leaders skillfully blended into a landscape of troops.

An organization headed up by one fella, or in this remarkable instance, two fellas, is already in trouble, according to Stone thinking. Somehow the screws are going to identify the leaders and bust them. Bust goes the organization. But with lots of leaders, scattered in among the general run of fellas, the screws are not going to know at any time whether or not they have busted the right guys. The screws are going to be discomfited, in fact, because after they have satisfied themselves they *did* bust the right guys, to the amazement of all, the resistance keeps chugging along. The exigencies of prison life demanded that set-up. Decisions were conciliar. Policy was set by groups of leaders, the very ones, in fact, who were charged with carrying it out. Feedback was built in, apparently, because there are recollections of some resistance operations which were busted by the organization, in the moment that ordinary rank-and-file members refused to go along with the leaders.

One should not assume that the organization developed in St. Charles was as elaborate or as far-reaching as the eventual Blackstone organization. One can safely assume, though, that the eventual organization which developed on the streets was embryonically portended by the St. Charles organization. Furthermore, what developed on the streets did not go beyond the embryonically declared lines of the St. Charles organization. In this sense, one can say Blackstone has not got out of prison to this day.

The organization was designed to work under conditions of insuperable difficulty. It was not formed in order to while away hours of idleness. These particular incorrigibles did not band together for the purpose of letting off a little steam, either in the form of delinquent acts of libidinal drainage. They were banded together already, before they got to the streets, in the brotherhood of resistance which could count among its successes the endurance of rehabilitation.

Resist the authorities! Of course. Not just any authorities, or some authorities, or all authorities in some mindless ideological way. Resist those authorities which try to break you with force. The prison has lots of ways of hurting prisoners, and some of them belong to a species of psychological warfare, but all depend on the gun, the rubber hose, and the fist. This is the authority prisoners resist. It is an authority of violence. It announces, "You have no rights. You have no place in society. You are criminal. You will not even have any being if you don't watch out." This is what the Stones call "the system." They do not mean racism, oppression, intolerance, discrimination, or prejudice. They have little use for such abstract and high-sounding matters. By "the system" they mean this particular way the "man" has of arranging himself, with instruments of violence in his hands, telling you to do what he says. When he gets himself together like that, and looks a kid hard in the eye, as if to beat him or shoot him with the eyes alone, the kid does not ask inside himself the question of whether or not he should obey. The "man" has thrown the entire question of right and wrong into neutral by standing there like that. He could not possibly ask the kid to do something which would be right for the kid to do. The "man" is already wrong and anything he demands from the kid is wrong. What the Stones mean by "the system" is, precisely, corrupt, sadist authorities, inside and outside St. Charles. The pre-Rangers had been knowing the "system" that gathered itself into theretofore unknown concentrations of meanness. The continuous factor was meanness, whether focused or diffuse. So, one sees, their understanding of the "system" is not restricted to St. Charles. The "system" is no less than the America they had been on the receiving end of since birth.

They had seen no other America. Since they neither read nor traveled, they had no way of discovering there might be something else. So, at this early date, they did not make the short step from the idea of a hated system, encountered in boyhood and summarized by St. Charles, to the idea of two different kinds of America, the one they knew and the other. Some experience of another America would have to intervene before such an idea could possibly arise. And it did.

As they came out of St. Charles, they were convinced of the idea that America (i.e., the America they knew) is a jail in pretty much the same way St. Charles is a jail. They had gone from one jail, Woodlawn, to another jail, St. Charles, then returned to the Woodlawn jail.

And they didn't even realize the novelty of the idea! They were unaware that anyone might find that a shocking statement, or that some people might not understand themselves to be cons and the police, screws.

It has become considerably more pedestrian. The likening of the ghetto to a jail has, since 1965, become fashionable among black-power intellectuals and is a standard feature of new left rhetoric. This fact may tend to minimize the importance of Blackstone's idea in 1960! Blackstone did not hear the idea at a rally or read it in a book. It was their own idea. More than an idea, it was the linch-pin in their world-view, such as it was. To understand, then, their enormous capacities for violence no less than their defiant resistance to the police, this initial idea must be first understood.

Understanding is difficult because of the complications which arise. Blackstone said "Woodlawn is a jail" and meant "for us," that is, Blackstone and Blackstone-type people. I haven't found any evidence to suggest that they considered all Woodlawn people as prisoners. Quite to the contrary, they counted most of the residents of the community as part of the system, hence as guards, aligned in Blackstone's thinking with the police. Manifestly, Woodlawn is *not* a jail for most of the residents. It surely is not a jail for all the agency workers in the welfare offices, youth commission offices, YWCA offices; Woodlawn is not a jail for the policemen in the third district or for the employees of city, county, and state governments who live in Woodlawn (otherwise called "patronage workers"); Woodlawn is not a jail for schoolteachers, principals, administrators in Public School District Fourteen; Woodlawn is not a jail for the merchants, wireroom operators, dope-pushers and other fortunately employed people, many of whom have a "deuce and a quarter" parked in front of the apartment to prove it; Woodlawn is not a jail for ministers, social workers, leaders of community organizations, the newspaper editor, and his reporters.

These people are deeply offended by the statement that Woodlawn is a jail. It is a poor community. It is underprivileged. It is a ghetto.

But to call it a jail is a slur, and probably subversive. As a matter of historical record, what upset them most in the Blackstone assertions was the gall of delinquent kids undertaking to speak for the whole community, although that was not Blackstone's intention. The A-number-one, charging-ahead leaders of the community then undertook to speak for the whole community, including the delinquent kids. It would be amusing were it not so cruel. In contesting a point Blackstone never made, they displayed the empirical certitude of the point. They acted like jailers. They said everything is okay around here and promptly urged harder police action.

Bob Keeley, a First Church staff worker, monitored a meeting sponsored by the Woodlawn Boys Club in 1966. The meeting had been called to air differences which had arisen in the local high school. Representatives of the administration were there, of course, as well as student-body spokesmen, and police-department representatives. Throughout the meeting the students attacked the administration for allowing policemen in the halls as guards. The students claimed the policemen did more violence than they were put there to stop. Spokesmen for the school flatly denied the insinuation. At one point an assistant principal, obviously agitated, said, "I demand you produce evidence of police brutality; it is not true that policemen have abused students." Every adult in the room, says Bob Keeley, nodded in agreement. Bob also noticed that as soon as the school official had asked for evidence, a hand shot up on the back row. Now this was a curious hand, because it was in a cast. So, as the adults were nodding away in agreement, all of the students in the room began to laugh. This was disconcerting to the school official because he thought the students were laughing at something he had said, which they were, in a way. They were laughing because the official would not recognize the young man waving his hand-in-a-cast so vigorously on the back row. The joke was on the official. The hand, Bob shortly discovered, had been broken by a police baton not a week before the meeting. The young man was not trying to get the floor in order to make a speech. He was producing the evidence asked for, and the assistant principal was so bound up in the agreement procedures among the adults he didn't even see it. The students thought of it as preordained.

"Woodlawn as a jail" occurs in a sphere of the community the leaders do not know, such as the corner of 63rd Place and Blackstone Avenue. A five-year-old boy stands there throwing stones as hard as he can at every car going by and at all people who approach him. Before this area was demolished by urban renewal it ranked as one of the most degraded single living areas in the world, vying with the worst to be found in Recife, Calcutta, Hong King, or Harlem. One should not pause to document this boy's marginal starvation or his chronic anemia. One would be thought a bleeding heart. One should not expect to find bad teeth or be disconcerted at the flimsy clothing he is wearing on such a cold and windy day, either, for the same reason. The boy shows the undisguisable marks of having been beaten repeatedly, recently, and vigorously. His family has beaten him; older children in his family and the neighborhood beat him the day before in a contest for the use of a partially wrecked tricycle. This little boy knows what violence is. He has seen it happen to him. But he has seen plenty of violence happening to other people, too. He has seen street fights since he was old enough to begin remembering. A whore house and wireroom overlook his "play" area. He knows the intimate sound of a .38 caliber revolver being fired at close range. He is acquainted with the shapes of unknown running men. He knows the no-sound of a knife slashing human flesh. He is acquainted with the slow red ooze of blood as it first begins to show through clothing. He is a pro when it comes to violence.

This little boy has begun attending school. He hasn't the social imagination to realize he is already a candidate for the dummy room. Without intending it, he has already inflamed the teacher against him; she has had him marked from the first day as a trouble-maker and already is persuaded he is severely retarded. It would make little difference to him, but it is nonetheless a fact already that he shall never be permitted into the best classrooms of an atrociously second-class school. He is a dummy in the Scott Elementary School where he will probably learn to read and write his name after enduring the required seven years of banality and cruelty before convention says he can drop out. He has never seen inside a magazine or newspaper. Only on a half dozen lucky occasions has he watched TV; he has never held a book in his hands. He once got a truck for Christmas and it was stolen that day.

Here he is hurling stones at cars and people. He is angry. His revenge has swollen into a fury. Since all parts of his universe careen whimsically into him and hurt him, he has no recourse. He will fight back. And were his mother or a saint of the Church of God to appear, he would not moderate his attack. This in fact did occur. A true saint, Father Tracy O'Sullivan, appeared, suffering the stones in astonishment. In relating this incident, Father O'Sullivan recalled his immediate awe at the force of hopeless rage in one so young.

Is not the main meaning of a prison the fact one cannot get out? Then what miracle could be imagined on an order huge enough to extricate this boy from his destiny? Already he is wrong. He was wrong for going to the trouble of being born. He was wrong to have been born with black skin into an already too-large family. He must be wrong to have been slapped around so much. The verdict of his teacher makes it unanimous. Had he any doubts, she removed them.

In this throwing stones at cars and people he is showing definite antisocial trends, to say nothing of violating the property rights of his fellow ctiizens. And he must not be allowed to persist in this proto-criminal activity. He must be taught, as young as he is, that a fellow cannot get away with that kind of behavior. So he will be slapped around some more. And with absolute certainty, he will hate the further violation of his being. He will slowly become a dedicated wrongdoer. One day soon he will be taken up by his older brothers and helped to see he has been right all along, but that the adults, the authorities, the screws are wrong. Irresistibly jail beckons! Yes, he will soon enough be in a literal jail, glaring at literal guards. Then he will know the meaning of his life.

The community leaders do not speak for this child when they insist Woodlawn is merely a poor ghetto community. They speak against him and become a part of the jail he has been sentenced to. There are many other children—many other Woodlawn youth and adults—just like him.

During the years 1965–71, the staff of the day school maintained by First Church came into intimate contact with hundreds of Woodlawn families. Some of them were comfortable, aspiring, and healthy —although poor. Most of them were found to be on the brink of disaster, *perpetually.* The disaster kept coming at them. As Tom Lehrer maliciously sings, they were "sliding down the razor blade of life." It is not periodic hunger, or generally bad health, *or* the obvious marks of violence in the home which exactly characterize these families. They are in a self-duplicating cycle of environmental deprivation. More simply put, they can't get out, they know it, and in attempting the mere tasks of staying alive inside this fortress of impossibility they repeatedly fail. No psychological description of their depression quite catches the indicated meaning of ceaseless hand-wringing in mothers, or the immutable hostility of the children. Their suppressed rage is negatively transcended by a deeper hopelessness—of *ever* getting out. The files in the school office contain the material substance of prison life as family after family has come to disclose the true meaning of being barred by flaming machine guns from entering the yonder Eden of mere opportunity.

One should not consider this an excessive use of language for effect. The machine guns are intended to be understood as the symbolic representatives of the plethora of instruments of violence displayed daily and used daily on Woodlawn streets by the police. It is the estimation of many of the people in Woodlawn that there is no such thing as police brutality, since they do not recognize it as brutality. They have known nothing else. Police brutality requires a standard from which to judge that some actions are brutal. Without such a standard—furnished by law and norms of police activity in other areas of the city and nation—how could the notion of brutality arise? These people see the guns, and observe the violent flurries of police fists and blackjacks in their alleys—against whom is of little concern, since it might be unwise to observe too carefully. They know nothing else. If they noticed, they might be amused by the slogan painted on all Chicago police squad cars, "We serve and protect."

The Stones, certainly, are not outraged by police brutality. This is normal. It is what guards do. The guards are merely doing their best to break you and you are merely resising all of the way. For this reason, perhaps, the Stones display a casualness bordering on nonchalance about being sent to jail. It is nothing to Blackstone. As First Church began to build its legal defense effort the staff came to know quite a lot about actual Stone arrests, indictments, trials, and sentences. They didn't know close to everything, but they knew about the definite Stones who had been sentenced to jail. The staff didn't know about all the others who just got sent to jail without the staff knowing about it. Consequently there would come times when a Stone would stop showing up at the church. The staff would ask where he was and would get no good answers. Then at an indefinite later time, the Stone would show up again. He would saunter in and ask, "What's happenin?" as though he had been there the day before. The Stones talked *endlessly* among themselves about who was in, for what, when they were getting out, since that was a part of their business. But they did not talk to the staff about such matters. Possibly there was as much Stone business going on inside as outside the jail. At any rate, it was no big deal, as they say. They didn't rage and fume around at the terrible system of injustice which wrongly took away their liberty. What liberty? When did they ever have any liberty?

The sound of urbanologists growling and lashing their tails must by now have created something like a clamor inside one's head. They are avowed enemies of such effortless Stone simplism and the parochialism it involves. Moreover, they are capable of explicating each incident of environmental deprivation in more complex terms. To summarize, what they find especially wrong with the Stone view is that it is a mere perception, which, when supported with powerful peer-group affirmation leads the deprived to further economic and social passivity. This view has the effect, then, of bolting a door which was not *necessarily* closed. The ghetto residents look upon a door *they* have bolted and liken their situation to being in jail. It is a misfortune that police and pariah groups feud with each other; it is equally unfortunate that ghetto residents resort so steadily to violent solutions to social conflicts.

One must attend to this criticism because it assumes an ordering of social fact on the basis of the widest possible consideration of relevant data. It is the opposite of a parochialism. The Woodlawn experience is seen as an item within the totality of American experience. From such a vantage point it could well appear that the people *imagining* themselves to be in an *apparent* jail have restricted their manner of looking at the horizon of opportunity. It could as well appear that the unfortunate feud which has developed between ghetto residents—notably Blackstone—and the police has been brought on by the formation of pariah groups, which, in turn, are the result of and produce environmental deprivation. Were the pariah groups to disband and get on with the fundamental social and economic business, the feud would vastly moderate. No doubt such an outcome could be looked for were only the pariah groups to develop a sufficiently broad experience out of which an enlightened decision could be made.

Thus, why don't they have the broad experience? Why do groups form in such a way as to earn a "pariah" reputation? Why is the horizon of opportunity so restricted? And what might be designed in the way of a social convulsion so sweeping that first vision would broaden and, following that, opportunity? One thinks of vastly upgraded public education; adequate medical care; more professional law enforcement; pleasant housing; occupational preparation; wholesome recreation; abandonment of parochially discriminatory employment policies. In such fashion, one sees, could the remedy to limited vision and opportunity be applied, the total cost of which would probably not exceed one billion dollars. The institution of the remedies does not lie within the capabilities of the ghetto sector, languishing as it is in poverty and parochialism. The remedies are the province of the sector which the Blackstone Rangers persist in seeing as the jail-*ers.* Let the jailers set about these remedies, and it could possibly be said that there would be no jail because the jail would have been torn down. But until the remedies are applied, one gains very little by questioning the authenticity of Blackstone's *mere* perception.

Woodlawn appears *at* the Stones, as a prison; it *intends itself toward* the Stones, as a prison. R. D. Laing has said: "The greater need there is to get out of an intolerable position the less chance there is of doing so. The more untenable a position is, the more difficult it is to get out of it."* This is the ghetto version of Catch-22. You can always escape except when you make the effort. The idea that Woodlawn is a jail is a subjective judgment, a function of mere perception. There is no final evidence to sustain it, since it is a manner of looking. That adolescent black people did develop such a manner of looking is a statement of fact, however. It was the beginning of a world-view which was finally expressed with the adoption of the "out" nation within the American nation view. Considerable intellectual energy went into the formulation of the idea; more courage was displayed in maintaining its validity against the prissy criticism of hordes of well-to-do and aspiring black and white neighbors. In its first surfacing into public view, Blackstone disdained the ordinary poor-mouthing language of ghetto hustlers. Blackstone was not crying for a place in the beloved America. Blackstone said, "Let us out of this goddamn jail or we tear it down." Such an uncompromising analysis had not been heard in Chicago. Little imagination is required to foresee the response such a moralist summons would invoke. The answer would be clear: "These could not be Americans talking; these are, after all, criminals." Which seems to be Blackstone's point.

* *The Politics of Experience* (London: Penguin Books, 1967), p. 26.

3 Overcome by the Overcomers

"Jail? What you talkin' about? Don't make no difference in or out; whole thing's jail far's you can see." This is the Stone way of saying hell-no; it is, in fact, a rebellion against "the way it's been around here too long." It is active resistance—a risky business particularly suited to daring young men whose *passion* equips them with a lust to defy. "The energy which builds fraternal organization is in rebellion against the family and the father; it is youthful energy. . . . [It] has that exuberance which overflows the confines of elementary necessity, and rises above labor into the higher, or is it the lower, sphere of play."* Norman O. Brown penetrates the snot of Chicago politics with one flashing blow of his insight. These younger brothers of Blackstone revolted *exuberantly* against the old way, elementary necessity, "always havin' to take it," and "always havin' to yassa the polices." They made resistance a game for the brave to play, a psychological shootout more intense than the real, and more devastating to the loser since manhood was made an issue more important than living.

Only literalist political schemers would see Blackstone as a community organization when it is so clearly a brotherhood of brigands, fugitives, felons, no-goods, and cast-offs. The teacher spotted them as they first walked into the room, their mothers before, and the authori-

*Norman O. Brown, *Love's Body*, (New York: Random House, 1966), pp. 13, 4.

42

ties soon after. Troublemakers, hellions, incorrigibles every one cast themselves by incantation and secret rites into a fraternity of "the new way." Under eerie green and red light, blackness became sweet. Tales of their violence make children whimper and grown men wet their pants. One can neither romanticize nor glorify them for they exist in a self-made aura of romantic understanding and glorify themselves endlessly. "The mighty men of Blackstone," they call themselves. "The Almighty Black P. Stone Nation," they say, as though the very words were magical. No more elementary necessity—nigger kid for them. "That jive's done for, dad."

But the political schemers had good eyes and ears. They came to the odd conclusion that Blackstone is a community organization because Blackstone took the initiative in appointing itself the guardian of the community. Here is what Blackstone said in public:

The peoples out here needin' protection. Lotta mean shit goin down every day. We ain't givin' 'em some oily-mouth snake talk like them leeches at urban progress [Urban Progress Center = the O.E.O. outpost in Woodlawn] always comin' around with program this and project that. Hell, they nothin' but—how do you call it?—parasites. Yah. That's what they is, they's parasites livin' *off* the peoples insteada helpin' 'em. They make their bread by takin' down the peoples' names and puttin' the names on papers and passin' the papers around and down to the loop so more parasites down there can look at the names on the papers. Some more parasites down there put the names on *their* papers and pass'em back down here so's the parasites down here can read about'em and go have a look if they still be the same peoples. Sure nuff, they not goin' to make no bread less'n there be peoples there who got names to put on their papers and stick in the files. No help atall. Detectives's that way, too, layin five dollar on some dude to get'im to tell lies on a brother. We gonna protect the peoples from all that kinda shit.

The more that statement is pondered the less clear it seems. Who are the peoples? The Woodlawn community on hearing the news that Blackstone was going to assume responsibility for its protection treated the announcement as an onrushing catastrophe. There is the confusion. Blackstone did not mean the Woodlawn community. Blackstone said and meant the "peoples." And peoples are whom

Blackstone knows, comes from, and *is:* hypes, winos, hookers, banged-up little kids, distracted half-mad mothers, hustlers, roustabouts, cons, men on the lam, pimps, runners, blind, sick, crazy, hungry and not hardly any old people because these peoples do not ordinarily live long enough to grow old. Blackstone's peoples are a pile of cast-offs, whom the regular poor call "bad niggers" for the reason they will really slit your throat. Blackstone could not confuse these people with the regular community because the regular community immediately assures itself there could be no confusion. I mean the regular poor are the regular community.

The regular poor can be seen before daybreak walking to the bus and "el." They must start to work at this early hour because they work in faraway white places and their shifts begin early. Soon the night workers will be in the same streets on the way home from the bus and "el." They try to have a decent home for their children; they work hard; when possible both father and mother work in order to save enough money to get out of the ghetto. To Stone peoples the regular poor are trying to be "fine American ladies and gentlemens," with their grand $5,500 a year regular money coming in. Stone peoples are as remote from regular poor as regular poor are from aspiring regular lower middle class. So Stone peoples know they don't belong to the regular poor community, and, furthermore, *never will.* They are the true wretched of the city, whom the words "black poor" tend to leave out. And these are the peoples the heated-up Blackstone warriors so earnestly started to protect. Only Blackstone could see they needed protection because Blackstone had not stopped being lower-than-poor peoples themselves who attract punishment and misfortune as their sores draw flies.

Urgencies produce the Black P. Stone Nation. Exuberance. Violence. Rebellion. The assembling of the Nation was at the same time a rallying of the outcasts, and enemies beware. "We's not *in* your fuckin' country; don't mess with us."

One recalls an apparently similar outbreak from W. E. B. DuBois.

It is difficult to let others see the full psychological meaning of caste segregation. It is as though one, looking out from a dark cave in the side of an impending mountain, sees the world passing and speaks to it; speaks courteously and persuasively, showing them how these entombed souls are hindered in their natural movement, expression, and development; and how their loosening from prison would be a matter of not simply courtesy, sympathy and help to them, but aid to all the world. One talks on evenly and logically in this way but notices that the passing throng does not even turn its head, or if it does, glances curiously and walks on. It gradually penetrates the minds of the prisoners that the people passing do not hear; that some thick sheet of invisible but horribly tangible plate glass is between them and the world. They get excited; they talk louder; they gesticulate. Some of the passing world stop in curiosity; these gesticulations seem so pointless; they laugh and pass on. They still either do not hear at all or hear but dimly, and even what they hear they do not understand. Then the people within may become hysterical. They may scream and hurl themselves against the barriers, hardly realizing in their bewilderment that they are screaming in a vacuum unheard and that their antics may actually seem funny to those outside looking in. They may even, here and there, break through in blood and disfigurement, and find themselves faced by a horrified, implacable, and quite overwhelming mob of people frightened for their own existence.*

Pointing to his colored brothers and sisters, DuBois called them "prisoners" of "caste segregation," "entombed," he said, in a "cave." He meant *all* his brothers and sisters. But that is exactly *not* what the Stones mean. They are describing something lower than colored existence, suffering a double blow, first from segregat*ing* society, then from the segregat*ed* society. The Stone peoples would fit in some dungeon to the rear of and beneath Dubois's cave.

Of course segregation put them there. Of course the police enforce the segregation, but no such simple explanation is going to find them or what they represent. They are the dregs of a racism issue; they are the residue of the caste-segregation issue. As if to prove it, the Stones smash down the wicked idea that they are merely underprivileged Americans. This is the passion in their defiance. Recall Jeff's speech to the Princess.

*W. E. B. DuBois, *Dusk of Dawn*, (New York: Schocken Books, 1968), pp. 130–1.

. . . So what we gonna do? We gonna have our own govament, the way our daddies did long time back. And what peoples get messed up by the polices and such is gonna be our peoples. They don't let us in their govament, we git our own. They not let us *in,* we be OUT. In some kinda super way. We be the *out* boys for the *out* peoples. . . .

This was not a manner of speaking or a show of fancy talk. Jeff intended it as a statement of fact, both comprehensive and blunt. Here are a group of people born and raised in America who claim they do not belong in America. Unlike some young men who recently renounced their citizenship and took up residence in Canada, these people say they have been renounced. They are not using the occasion of some monumental injustice to declare a secession; they are convinced they have been seceded *from.* No one consulted them in the matter of their nonplace in the nation. The decision was made—and, to hear them tell it, is repeatedly being made—by true American others. Americans have ruled them out, thrown them out, and keep them out.

Blackstone's recommendation to the outcasting America—"Don't mess with us"—is cryptic if intended as a complete recommendation. It seems to be a pledge that the Blackstone warriors will defend their nonplace, such as it is, and won't give another inch. It seems to be a warning as well. "Don't do any more of what you've been doing all along because we won't tolerate it." Taken as an inevitability that things could get no better, they seem to mean, "We are determined to see that things get no worse." The prison ethos can be seen shining through the recommendation. No mutuality exists between Blackstone and Blackstone's peoples (prisoners) and America (guards). "Your business is to watch us. Our business is to resist."

Where are the programs? What does Blackstone say should be done? These questions arise spontaneously, almost out of habit. I have heard them asked by bemused reporters or hostile police as if they were no questions at all, seriously intended to seek from Blackstone's own lips its ideas of what should and can be done. The questions arise as assertions of the utterly negative position Blackstone is in. And they are true assertions. Blackstone *is* in a negative position, the truth of which is readily confirmed by defensiveness and hostility. To make sure that things get no worse is a conservative position as well as desperate. But one should also see it will be a difficult pledge to keep, for things tend to get worse, and efforts to resist the flow of "elementary necessity" require all of the negativity heroes can muster.

It is to this elementary necessity I now want to turn. Elementary necessity is no less than the America Blackstone so defiantly says it is out of. This America is focused at times as a specific Chicago-America but is as large as the land. America *necessarily* is offended by the lower-than-poor and *necessarily* will take action against them, the better to subdue and erase, if possible, the offense which they constitute. America has already demonstrated what it will necessarily do. One need not suppose what it might do, or use a prophetic future tense, "America *will* take such and such an action. . . ." The record has already been written. Elementary necessity does not endure passively the sullen shouts of the lower-than-poor— whether they be the unorganized lower-than-poor in every American metropolis or the organized lower-than-poor, represented by the Black P. Stone Nation in Chicago. Elementary necessity does something. The procedures, as we shall see, are at best haphazard and at worst grotesque. But *something* is *necessarily* done.

For a brief period, 1960 through the first half of 1968, America really heard about the black poor. In fact, the national airwaves were glutted with talk about the black poor. For an even briefer period, 1965 through the first half of 1968, the general talk about the black poor seemed to include, of all things, concrete mention of the existence of the lower-than-poor. When Martin Luther King "came to Chicago," for instance, he promised to break the very walls of the ghetto down. This was in 1965. He meant all of the walls, including the final walls deep inside the ghetto which keep the Stone sort of peoples from participating in black poverty. Similar voices joined his in raising a national clamor about this outrage. Were all people born in this country, no matter what *color,* going to be included all the way into the real country with full rights, opportunity, freedom of movement, political participation—the "works"? This was what the clamor was made of. A constitutional question was being vigorously pressed upon a constitutional democracy. It meant: Would the nation own up to its racism and correct the injustices it produced?

Those were heady days for the semirightless, even the radically rightless. The nation was having to open up because it was getting a bad conscience from these smooth black people always on television telling the ugly story of "caste segregation." For a specific three-year period it was possible to confuse that story with Blackstone's story and, strange to tell, to count Blackstone Rangers among Chicago civil rights organizations in some mysterious fashion. The police department's first suspicions about Blackstone Rangers were aroused when Rangers met with Dr. King and his colleagues in the spring of 1966. For a while it was possible to imagine that the general constitutional question had been stretched out so far that it covered colored brigands. Are *these* people Americans, too? On the panel shows during this brief era first the smooth black people would complain about discrimination in employment, housing, education. Then the rotten people, who during this era were actually seen on television, would begin their obviously *paranoid* talk about police brutality and *rats*— thus making a shambles of the shows. It looked as though these lower-than-poor might really make it into some kind of momentary indismissibility for the first time. It was (wistfully) hoped at any rate. Two of my colleagues at First Church attended a meeting of the Blackstone Rangers during the high tide of such hope and were startled to hear the Rangers attempt the first stanza of the "Star-Spangled Banner"—to the limited extent the Rangers were acquainted with it. That may be taken as an indication of how high hopes were then running. The hope, quite simply, was for continued recognition in a non-American status, not eventual inclusion in America. They had not gone insane.

The brief period came to a close. The lower-than-poor as a part of the constitutional question sank back out of sight. Blackstone Rangers got their honorary membership in the civil rights movement snatched off their jackets. Civil rights victories did them in. "We shall overcome," sang the civil rights movement. And they did—overcome the lower-than-poor. America started opening up to black Americans. Ironically, when black Americans won, the lower-than-poor lost. This is a complicated irony played out in recent national history which deserves more than casual mention.

The civil rights controversies of the entire period produced gains for black Americans. First, racial prejudice can no longer function automatically. The civil rights movement had identified it specifically. It still does function, of course, but not effortlessly. The civil rights movement continues to exist as a movement now dedicated to obstructing the effects of racial prejudice—caste segregation.

Considering the odds against its success, the movement's achievement is little short of miraculous. The movement has pointed out prejudice in American institutions, politics, industry, professions, armed forces, churches, neighborhoods, schools, and souls. Alongside a pretty sorry contemporary performance the movement placed the amassed evidence of 400 years of the same thing. How could the charges be rebutted? They were obviously true.

This gain is not only solid, it is apparently irrevocable. Unless racial prejudice turns itself into genocidal lust, it will never be able to operate out in the open again, or automatically. For the many long-suffering victims of caste segregation who now have been emancipated from its more obvious effects, this gain is at the same time a tremendous victory.

The second gain is equally substantial. Talented black Americans can participate in the conventionally prosperous American experience in numbers that a pre-1960 realist would have considered impossible. At this very minute black professionals are competing with white professionals for the top dollar in the top job. The expansion of the black middle class has been even more spectacular. Middle-level employees are making and spending middle-level money at a *fantastic* rate. Black capitalism is still a myth but black entrepreneurs are not a myth. They exist. They have not been picking cotton out in the hot sun, either. They know the difference between the black market and the American market. They are tooling up to get their share of the big market. Then black capitalism will not be a myth any more.

There are not many black professionals, not many more middle-class employees, or black entrepreneurs. But there are a lot more than one could reasonably have expected a decade ago. Their children are growing up in relative affluence, and have never known that they do not have lots of opportunity. They are blessed with normal competitive endowments. It is not unreasonable to expect that they will go much further upward than their parents have.

This gain is also irrevocable. One cannot imagine Bill Cosby's children ever being niggers.

The two gains were won in a contest. They were the subject of bloody controversy. Neither white nor black racists were willing to yield them cheaply. White racists wanted to restrict the American experience of untrammeled upward mobility to white people. They were not alone in contesting black success. Black racists didn't like the idea either. The American dream was working too well to suit them. They wanted to maintain that *all* black people presently endure a slavery as remorseless and apparent as the slavery from which they were but technically emancipated in 1863. Such a position is confounded by all of the black success which was going on. Neither of the racist apologetics slowed down the process. Black people were succeeding. The melting pot was bubbling away just like the most sentimental ninth-grade social-studies teacher says it does.

A talented and aggressive black young person today looks ahead to a world of reward based on merit not color. He will have to be more talented and pursue his goals more agressively than the white young person with whom he will be competing, but he has a chance to win the competition. His children's chances will be improved the more he wins. Although condemned by black-power theoreticians as another deplorable tokenism, or, worse, the newest version of paternalism, black American gains are *gradualism*. This is not a gradualism ruthlessly chopped down root and branch but a gradualism whose roots and branches are positively thriving! Characteristically, the civil rights movement demanded freedom, equality, full dignity for all black people—NOW! The gradualism it saved its bitterest condemnation for, it got.

The civil rights movement cannot be fairly blamed because the controversies it provoked benefited the majority of black people so little. The record is clear. The movement entered the struggle in behalf of the poor, untalented, and powerless little people. As a prophet to the nation it presented the plight of the unfranchised, plantation-southern, urban, marginally starving, badly schooled, rat-bitten, lynched, mutilated, abused, ignored, poor black folks. The nation responded with a loose translation of its motto: "Give me your talented, prepared, smooth, and unhungry." Gradualism *is* elementary necessity. It is elementary for the nation to say, "Why deal with *lumpen*black when we have—*Julian Bond?* Send us all the Julian Bonds you've got." It is also elementary for the nation to believe that its ready acceptance of great, *swinging,* black people has automatically fixed up the plight of the others. Newly successful black Americans obscure the fact that no change has occurred where the civil rights movement called most insistently for change.

The owner of a swank apartment house would likely be sued were he to deny occupancy to black tenants, because they have the money to pay for the lease and to sue. This fact obscures the other fact, that the owner of a slum building gouges his black tenants with as little difficulty as he did in 1959. Similarly, a star baseball player, Rico Carty, was beaten by Atlanta policemen. Atlanta had become so enlightened about such things in 1971 that Mr. Carty just charged into the mayor's office and demanded his rights. And the mayor agreed! The policemen were promptly fired and must stand trial for assault. But an unemployed black youth in the same city, suffering the same abuse (or worse) finds his case as hard to make as ever and perhaps harder. Good Atlanta burghers take such satisfaction in attending to Mr. Carty's rights they imagine all black people now roar into the mayor's office if they are abused.

One will note in the relentless acceptance of Julian Bond that there is a corresponding retreat of the lower-than-poor from public view. *Necessarily.* This is what gradualism means. Far from obscuring the plight of the black *poor,* it exposes them to ranges of hope virtually as wide as America itself. With successful black Americans already pioneering the way, an invitation has been offered to the black poor: "In time, you, too, can make it; yes, you, poor as you presently are, can one day make it into the land of comfort and plenty. Hungry as you now are, you will one day eat so well your dogs will grow fat on the leftovers. Stand up for yourselves; you can overcome." The American dream dreams itself. On being born, an American (thoughbeit black and poor) is entitled to a place in the American scheme. A person will prosper according to his talents and luck. The fortunate experience of some current black Americans helps to promote the dream. People who find very humble places in the scheme are *(a)* improperly motivated; *(b)* untalented; *(c)* lazy; *(d)* unlucky. But they do have a place—as the poor. With appropriate changes in *(a)-(d)* a better place can automatically be expected. A country cannot have all rich people, or even all affluent people, for there must be poor people as well. All are locked together, however, by the same hope of eventual success and greater success.

As a result of national decision, the black poor have been given a license to enter the race for success. Plight is removed and promise installed in its place. The black poor have color TV! They can feast their eyes on the merchandise offered them and they can feast their souls with an audacity to want it and work for it and eventually buy it. Gradualism has the particular effect of condensing impatience into resolve so that tomorrow's reward inspires today's performance. Once licensed as real Americans, the black poor have only to succeed. Nothing stands in the way. It is a matter of spirit alone. One believes. That is all there is to it. One becomes absorbed with belief. One's life begins to conform to the belief. Success is a belief which is the truest capital of all in the American scheme. What matter how many tomorrows intervene, or how success recedes from the pursuing believer when he moves to capture it? The promise drives him on.

To the precise extent gradualism assumes that *every* one is ruled into the scheme by birth, it is both reckless and untrue. Michael Harrington's *The Other Americans* is not so dated that it cannot be used by itself to destroy such an assumption. But gradualism doesn't make that assumption. Gradualism assumes something quite different. Every person is ruled in who *wants* to be in. A matter of will, one sees, of proper motivation. How could it be otherwise? America is not a welfare state. America was created by, is sustained by, and must continue to be nourished by people who want to do real social and economic business. Since a strictly spiritual belief is the crucial item which licenses the black poor to be actual Americans, its absence means *necessarily*—in the most elementary and absolute way—that unbelievers do not even appear in the American scheme.

By elementary necessity these *lumpen*black, lower-than-and-permanent-poor got shunted off out of sight by the very gestures of national decision to include the regular black poor into the run for the roses. They do not belong, necessarily. The irony arises just here. Their plight was the occasion for the national clamoring. The civil rights movement wanted recognition of their plight. Its most authentic train of thought, in fact, was the recurring comparison between the poor demonstrators and the police dogs chasing them. Civil rights preachers did not tire of pointing out that the police dogs were better fed, received better medical attention, were better housed, better schooled, and were accorded more respect than the so-called American citizens they had been trained to attack. It is a short distance to dogs in general. Hence it became a truism in civil rights rhetoric that the dogs of real Americans are treated better than vast numbers of the black poor.

But somehow, one notices, the most authentic and promising train of thought was lost in a clamor for instant rights, better laws, and good-faith guarantees. The people whose plight had produced the conscience-stricken national decision did not fit into that program at all. They were the issue, it seemed, which America necessarily turned into another issue. The victories of the civil rights movement would not have been so quickly or easily won had the most important primary issue been pressed, even to the detriment of lesser issues. Martin Luther King's brilliant speech before the Lincoln Memorial in Washington, D.C., in 1963 summarized the apparatus of the American dream. It has been praised by all manner of Americans who would not have been prepared to deal with any uncomfortable notions that millions of other people—some weird sub-Americans, perhaps—cannot get in on that dream. Such a reality was prudently muted. The praise accorded the speech shows the wisdom of such prudence, and justifies the earlier decision made by the various civil rights leaders to censor the remarks of John Lewis, then the number one S.N.C.C. organizer. Mr. Lewis did not believe in prudence. He wanted to talk about the dogs. He had, in fact, prepared a speech which attacked the pending administration civil rights legislation, because he thought there were more important prior matters to raise. He wanted to contest elementary necessity, gradualism, sell-out, fraud, hypocrisy. His question was all that Blackstone might have wished it to be: "Which America you-all talkin about?" The coalition of civil rights organizations almost fell apart right there over the Lewis speech. *Necessarily,* Mr. Lewis was forced to delete the imprudent sections of his speech, so that the large gathering of people, on which the largest concentration of national interest was focused, did not hear about all of those people languishing far below ever having the hope of beginning life guaranteed by Dr. King's American dream.

Inevitably, the national decision about its racial injustice—gradualism—had the direct effect of rendering a whole lot of people furnishing the plight ineligible for the victory party. Already lower-than-poor, hence sub-American, they became, for these reasons—astonishing!—subblack!

One begins to appreciate the anger which fuels resistance to such elementary necessity. Having been driven all their days into an active antimotivation, and finding motivation is the absolute prerequisite for beginning real American life, they cannot begin, and since beginning is what licenses even the black poor for true citizenship, the Stones and their people are judged unfit black people. The shape of a triple bind begins to appear—or, precisely, the complicated irony of having been overcome by the victorious civil rights overcomers.

Stones, Stone peoples in Chicago, their counterparts in all American cities continue to be the vexing problem they have always been, whether recognized or ignored. They are a perpetual mockery to the virtuous constitutional democracy humming away on every side of them. Even when they bestir themselves and seek to establish a reciprocity with regular Americans, as surely they did during the brief period when it seemed they were being covered by the movement's concerns, they are misunderstood, or worse, disputed. When they ask nothing except, "Don't mess with us," they are contested and messed with. One is staggered that there is any initiative at all. What might have possessed them to undertake dialogue with this domineering country which has cast them as alien-natives? What led them to believe the regular Americans all about them could understand the motifs of their resistance or decode the meaning of their violent deeds? These are hard questions and their answers would be helpful. But the questions can no longer be asked. They are not being raised now any more than they have been seriously raised since the civil rights movement caved in. No one could now be especially interested in the social convulsion which might be required to extend the felicities of constitutional citizenship even to Stone people. All of that has passed. Another era has been entered, marked by a new disaster.

Stones, Stone peoples, and their counterparts in all American cities have become, *necessarily,* Criminals! A new way of looking at them has appeared. And in the nick of time, too. Are not these the very people causing so much trouble all the time? Have they not fire-bombed cities, drained the welfare bank, destroyed normal life in the inner cities of the nation, killed policemen, menaced law-abiding citizens with theft, assault, murder, and rape? Of course. Why wasn't the matter seen that way from the start? Whatever could one have been thinking to have been even momentarily exercised over their possible rights as possible citizens? All along they have been a criminal problem. The policemen have been right. In such fashion sub-America becomes criminal America and can be safely passed over to the law-enforcement agency for action. There was a way all along to fit them into the American scheme, a way disguised by the distractions offered by bleeding hearts. You bet they *are* Americans—*bad* Americans who should be put in jail and made to find out that crime will not be tolerated in this country.

Between the decline of the sub-America issue in the priorities of the civil rights movement and this writing, it has re-emerged as an issue in law and order. The boundaries of sub-America, luckily, are the boundaries of the black criminal problem.

On September 29, 1968, Republican presidential candidate Richard Nixon made his first major speech on crime. "Some have said we are a sick society," he said, pointing backward to the agony of a disjoined country losing its war on poverty. Then he suggested a fresh way of looking at it. "We're sick all right, but not in the way they mean. We are sick of what has been allowed to go on in this nation too long." His brilliant facility with commonplace expression was never shown to greater advantage. He provided a simple, adequate, *final* way to look at the issue. He continued to speak, but he had no need to. He continued in following speeches to use the same words in that same miraculously simple combination, but needlessly. Once uttered, he accomplished the new way of looking. The lower-than-poor, sub-American, sub-black wretched of the country might well have felt a tremor as the words were spoken. It was their landscape shifting— from unnamable poverty to crime.

More to the point of this present study, Blackstone rarely has recommended itself to the people of Chicago in its own terms, although the terms are neither radical nor new. They would be troubling to Chicago if fully heard. The serious minded citizens of that city would be critically challenged by the fairly conservative Blackstone assertions about their life outside America while living here. But to my knowledge Blackstone could never make its case. When it emerged from its prisonlike secrecy and shadowy existence in the alleyways of the south side, it emerged as a hated and feared criminal gang. That designation was the way of looking which obliterated anything they might have to say. They were not passive-rotting-away poor people, but violent-bloody poor people. The violence obscured everything else, including their subpoverty, and, ironically, their fanciful claim of subcitizenship. Since the way of designation necessarily blanketed them with thorough disguise, policemen were required, not a final reckoning.

The attempts to curb black crime have proved a notorious flop.

Crime rates in what are euphemistically called "high-crime areas" are not going down. With all the fresh concentration of personnel, new equipment, and national concern mobilized to handle the top priority problem, black crime has blithely gone its own way, immune to the effort. A suggestion exists that the crime fighting is having the reverse effect of promoting crime. However that may be, enough evidence now exists to demonstrate that the problem is not directly a criminal problem, hence is not directly susceptible to solution by applications of ever higher ranges of force. One may easily imagine that residents in "high-crime areas" do not look upon what they do or what happens to them as crime. In their view they enjoy all of the punishments and are afforded none of the protections of the law. Here they are, systematically banished from poverty, America, and okay blackness, *and* here they are, systematically deluged with an occupation *army* of policemen who demand conformity to the law! Their question, accordingly, is rather bitter. "How can we be criminals if we are not even Americans?" The irony of the question is, of course, missed by the policemen.

One can scarcely imagine the full scope of this disastrous transformation from subpoverty to crime. The issues of the subpoverty are clearly primary because they recommend the view that America is not better and probably worse than South Africa. But once criminality is introduced as the reigning way to look at the issue, the primary matters can no longer emerge. The items of criminality are so everlastingly odious that their appearance tends to disguise everything else surrounding them. All one must do is raise them and they then disguise everything else, whether or not they are factually true. The possibility they *might* be true is sufficient to abort any other kind of discussion. Criminality as the issue produces a layer of controversy so thick the orginal issue becomes forgotten.

Few readers in America will need to be told at this late date that the Blackstone Rangers are a criminal gang or that Stone peoples are a "cesspool of criminality." As a consequence, few readers have had the opportunity to face the issues Blackstone raises and the issues they are. It is toward such a goal this study is directed. The basic matters will not languish in forced disguise. Blackstone has not passively accepted the weight of condemnation but has fought against it. These are historical facts, portentous almost beyond telling. But how can regular Americans understand these facts if the very gestures of the struggle are understood, *necessarily,* to be more evidence of criminality?

What I shall attempt to do, therefore, is penetrate the disastrous charge of criminality in order to come again to the subpoor, sub-American, sub-black starting point. It will be discovered that the starting point has changed because of the disaster. It seems that the new way of looking has produced something like a metamorphosis of the issue itself into a secondary form. And in that form it is highly unstable. Not only Blackstone but a great majority of their fellows in the same sub-American place, resist the designation. They do not forsake what is called crime. They forsake the law. The second metamorphosis—at once most perverse and dangerous—is the return of criminal as outlaw. This consideration will appear in due time. Its chilling presence here, as a premonition, emphasizes the importance of the work of rediscovery.

Part Two

Metamorphosis: Black Criminals

The defiant lower-than-poor are seldom encountered in their pure rage. A campaign has been launched against them aimed at transforming them into a criminal problem. The campaign provided America with a handy set of lurid perceptions which feature the lower-than-poor as thieves, murderers, thugs, specialists in violence, rapists, anarchists, and savages. The campaign is great PR, a brilliant success. The question of the lower-than-poor being outside a denying nation would be totally obliterated were not the campaign ironically to have displayed its truth.

4   The Mayor Declares War

. . . [Chicago State's Attorney Edward] Hanrahan, after the 1968 elections, declared war on the young black street gangs and on the Black Panther Party. The black gangs frightened Daley, and it wasn't because they shot at each other, or because some of them had commited murders in their membership drives, and wars over territories. One of the gangs, the Black P. Stone Nation, had grown to a looseknit membership of several thousand and was beginning to show signs of political and economic awareness and the use of such power. Black politicians were currying its favor, and private social agencies were making efforts to channel it into legitimate business activities. Daley had seen the same thing happen before. He recalled Regan's Colts, the Irish thieves and street fighters who became the most potent political force in neighboring Canaryville, and his own neighborhood's Hamburgs, who got their start in the same brawling way before turning to politics and eventually launching his career. There lay the danger of the black gangs. Blacks had been killing each other for years without inspiring any great concern in City Hall. But these young toughs could be dictating who their aldermen would be if he didn't stop them. And the Black Panthers, a more sophisticated though smaller group was even more dangerous. They had set up a free food program in the ghetto and had opened a health clinic that was superior to those of his own health department. The Police Department had already been applying constant pressure when Hanrahan came charging in with his personal war. The police Gang Intelligence Unit was, in fact, bigger than the unit assigned to crime

61

syndicate activities. But Hanrahan created a seperate unit of his own for the same purpose.*

The government of the City of Chicago takes the position that all inhabitants of the city are one of two and only two kinds, friend or foe, and under these alternate billings are also citizens of the republic who must abide within the law. If some people want to believe they are not American citizens, that is their opinion, on a par with opinions of crazy people who believe they are Napoleon or that the city will be invaded from outer space next Thursday afternoon. Whether friend or foe is not, however, an idle matter of opinion. The friend/foe scale is more important than all other scales, such as Democrat/Republican, rich/poor, and black/white. It is *the* operative dividing line. It may shift and thus appear arbitrary. It is. But it is never frivolously shifted. One of the many virtues of Mike Royko's book *Boss* is to make clear that the superintendent in charge of politics in Chicago— "the Boss," no less, Richard J. Daley himself—is the final arbiter of friend/foe arrangements, though not the only one thinking about such important matters. He is the leader of a city government whose primary task is to help friends and to hurt foes. Since it is a resourceful government, it can really help and really hurt. One finds it awful to fall into the hands of a living Daley as foe, but of the greatest beneficence to be counted as friend of his administration.

It could reasonably be expected, from provisional understandings of the Black P. Stone Nation, that these young men would not be worried about any additional disaster involved in becoming a foe of the Daley machine, and might have concluded by attending to the experience of their regular daily lives that they had always been a foe. Conceivably, they would welcome an open declaration of foeship from the mayor. Clearly, their world-view features Daley as the "king fuzz," as the "top screw." Nothing he might do to them could surprise them. They were set up to "give 'im fits," if he is "gonna act ole Charley's part." It was no disaster when the mayor and his counselors decided to land a few warning whacks on Ranger skulls, and when

*Mike Royko, *Boss* (New York: E. P. Dutton & Co., Inc., 1972), pp. 206, 207.

that didn't seem to produce the desired harmony, decided to wipe them out. To the Stones, this was "more jive piled on topa the old jive." One can agree it was "more," all right, and add, "a whole lot" more.

Whenever the decision was made, it surfaced as a public fact on May 9, 1969. The mayor, flanked by his protégé, State's Attorney Edward Hanrahan, appeared at a press conference to announce a "war on criminal gangs in Chicago." They announced the creation of a task force of gang experts drawn from all areas of city government, whose job it would be to work out a battle plan. The task force went to work right away. On August 4 the group released to all news media copies of a document entitled, "Organized Youth Crime in Chicago." This report was the battle plan. Internal marks—poor quality of reproduction, interlinear pencilings, incomplete references, typos, garbled passages—indicate the document was got to this releasable condition in haste, almost as if to say, "You must realize the problem this afternoon; another twenty-four hours taken to polish the thing up would make it too late." Furthermore, since when are gang experts also literary nuts?

This document is, perhaps, the "more jive" which Stones considered was being "piled on topa the old jive." At any rate, they consider it the most recent demonstration of the city's crazy hatred, not something new. I consider it a most important document. It marks the conclusion of a historical process which had been haphazardly begun in May, 1966. Between that time, when Blackstone was considered vague trouble, eligible for a little heat, "slap 'em around some," and the release of the report in August, 1969, Blackstone had steadily grown in negative public acclaim from trouble to bad trouble to organized trouble to malevolently organized trouble to criminals to organized criminals to—the end of the process—the number one problem facing Chicago, no less than "organized youth crime." As the process was transforming them into ever more ugly apparitions of evil, it was also systematically obliterating their contentions about "out" life in Chicago. The document marking the end of the process also shows the finished work of obliteration. There is no more residue to be found. Blackstone had become all "criminal gang."

The document is also interesting as a possible source of information about "jive." If Blackstone is correct in calling it "jive," the "game" the city is "switching" on them should be plain enough for the non-Blackstone human eye to see. One should be able to find out something about the otherwise secret mechanisms city government uses to confer foeship, *if* it is "jive." With such improbabilities in mind, let us attend without further comment to

The Report

The Black P. Stone Nation is encountered in "Organized Youth Crime in Chicago" as one of three major Chicago street gangs. It is accorded eighteen pages of description while the Disciples rate three paragraphs, along with the Vice Lords, who also rate three paragraphs. This possible discrepancy occurs "because the Rangers have become the largest gang in the city, and because their notoriety has led smaller gangs to emulate their violence and terror" (p. 11). The report may also at times be describing all gangs in general, but when doing so it is including the Rangers as the leading specimen of what a gang is.

Gangs became a problem in 1965, the report says. They expanded their ordinarily small numbers; they also increased the territories they each one pledged to protect. They thus went beyond their usual street-war rivalries. "Organized terror and violence were utilized for recruitment and discipline of gang members, and ultimately for the extortion of individuals and merchants in the gang's territory. Deadly force was increasingly used to achieve these ends" (p. 2).

The introduction opens with a police report of a species of this deadly violence.

At approximately 2000 hours, 23 April, 1968, the reporting police officers were assigned to "a boy shot." On arrival we learned the victim to be one Willis Clayton III, male, negro, age 16. The victim had sustained a bullet wound, the entrance of which was in the right rear of head and was embedded in front of left (brain) lobe. The victim succumbed from the bullet wound and was pronounced dead at 2035 hours, 23 April, 1968.

It is stated in the following paragraph: "Willis was finishing his freshman year at Dunbar when a teenage gang killed him. Gang members met him on the street and shot him in the head at point-blank range" (p. 1). This murder provides depth to the statistics soon offered. "From 1965–1969 over 290 persons have been slain in gang-related crimes. In 1967, the worst year of gang violence, over 150 people were murdered by Chicago gangs. In both 1967 and 1968 nearly 30% of those charged with murder were under the age of 21" (p. 2). A footnote to that reference adds: "In 1969 over 690 gang-related shootings were reported to the police. Nearly 70% of the victims were between 14 and 21 years of age. Sixty eight of the victims died."

In the section of the report devoted to the Blackstone Rangers, recruitment first is cited as an occasion for the use of deadly force. The Gang Intelligence Unit (GIU) supplied information that in May and June of 1966 sixteen youths were shot "because they were not members of the gang or refused to join. Thirteen more were beaten or stabbed" (p. 12). The report further states that "the Rangers shot 41 young people in their 1967 recruitment drive. Four died. One child was kidnapped and beaten. Thirty were beaten in the streets" (p. 13). The Rangers painted their names on "every" building in the heart of Woodlawn in order to "sustain fear and spread their reputation" (p. 13).

Gang discipline also produced occasions for the use of deadly force, according to the report. It notes that Cornell Steele has been convicted of the murder of James McCain in what the report states was "an assassination." Five other incidents are variously described in which Rangers used deadly force on other Rangers or one-time Rangers.

But the greatest occasion for the use of deadly force, says the report, was the Rangers' need to protect their territory against Disciples. "Due primarily to the warfare between the gangs, 19 teenage youths were shot to death in Woodlawn from September 1966 to September 1968. Approximately 150 Woodlawn youngsters were shot during the same period" (p. 18). A notation reveals, "This data was compiled from district files of the Chicago Police Department."

A typical case included in the report (p. 19) reads: "Earnest Rollins, 15-years-old and a Ranger, told homicide detectives of his combat experience":

"I opened up the gun to see if there were any bullets in it, and there were six bullets in it. I went toward Woodlawn and I saw a bunch of 'D's' standing on the corner of 65th and Woodlawn. Then I ran toward the alley so I could get a good shot, and then they started charging, and then I shot one of the boys. Then I looked to see if he was going to fall, and he fell. . . ."

Four other typical cases are included, after which the section on gang-rivalry-related shooting concludes:

The fact that more than 200 people, the majority in their teens, have been shot in Woodlawn in the past 3 years does not say enough. An injury from a bullet or shotgun blast puts a youth in the hospital, takes him out of school or work or possibly injures him forever. In the case of parents whose children are killed, it means the pain of the moment, identifying the dead child, the irreparable loss, and fear that it may happen to another child in the family (p. 22).

The report finds that recruitment expanded membership and dues. "The money went into the gang treasury and was used for such purposes as bail and guns" (p. 22). To dues was added the money which came from extortion. Five extortion attempts are described, after which this summary statement appears: "A total of 52 extortion complaints have been filed with the police where the accused has either identified himself as a Blackstone Ranger or is a known member of the gang" (p. 25). The report agrees with gang contentions that not everyone who identifies himself as a Ranger is a Ranger, but notes that these people "whether gang members or not, rely on the reputation of the gang for making good its threats" (p. 26).

The report places the Ranger participation in The Woodlawn Organization (T.W.O.) sponsored Job Training Project (funded by the

Office of Economic Opportunity) under the category of extortion. To substantiate this placement the testimony of a Disciple leader is adduced. He testified before a Senate investigating committee regarding $5-a-week kickbacks in Disciples' centers.

The project having been terminated, the Rangers, at the time of the writing of the report, had been forced to begin extorting businesses again.

In recent weeks several incidents have been brought to light which indicate that the Rangers are not neglecting this source of revenue. The owner of a tavern has left Woodlawn—and even the state for a period of time—as the result of an attempt by the Rangers to take over her establishment. In a statement to the police, she related that a Ranger told her he was assuming control of her tavern, and later said he was going to kill her. She left the state. The juke box dealer who supplied her tavern was subsequently visited by a group of six Rangers who demanded $125,000 to protect his business. The demand was later reduced to $50,000 (pp. 27–28).

Three other extortion incidents are described. In conclusion the report adds: "The Chicago police presently identify 32 young men as Ranger leaders. Among them they have more than 50 convictions for serious crimes and have served collectively more than 24 years in jail. Their crimes range from battery to murder" (p. 28).

There crime is in such volume and variety it is—sickening. Of course. That was the intent of the report. It was prepared for the purpose of alerting the people of the city to the menace of gang crime. It couldn't have been prepared for the enlightenment of city agencies; they prepared it. Inasmuch as the Blackstone Rangers are said to have done the things named in the report, they would not be especially edified either. The authors of the report released it to the news media, which promptly got the message out to the people.

Had the matter not been criminal gangs, some question might immediately arise about the manner of release. If, for instance, the corporate officers of a well-known Chicago industry had been the subject of the report, and their crime the particular point of the report

—both crime they have committed already and crime they are likely to go on committing—a reader might wonder why the report was not sent to the police and investigators of the state's attorney's office so that the crimes might be tried and the potential crimes averted. But this report was prepared exclusively from data supplied *by* the police and state's attorney's office. What is lacking in their existing authority and resources to get the criminals to trial? If they haven't enough money, the report might better be sent to the city council for emergency action. If they haven't sufficient personnel to get the job done, they might attempt to deputize some volunteers. The resources of both agencies, however, seem to be adequate. With the data-evidence right there, going on for page after page, why aren't they formulated into charges presentable to a grand jury? Or, is there something about the data-evidence which recommend the message form rather than the charge form?

The idea of substantial members of the business community being called a criminal gang by the mayor and state's attorney is beyond reason. It is unthinkable they could be made the subject of a report deliberately released to all news media. Why? Quite simply, because the subjects would sue the city for slander *and* libel, and would win the suit, unless the city was prepared to prove everything it said in the report to a court; at that, the subjects could probably prove malice directed against them in the fact that the proved statements were not *first* presented to the court.

But, then, these members of the Blackstone Rangers are not substantial members of the business community. Apparently they are substantially less possessed of rights than others in Chicago, or, at least, less possessed of the resources to press for their rights, which may amount to the same thing. And in that position, the question of slander did not present itself to the mayor and state's attorney or the question of libel to the authors of the report in sending the message out to the people.

The authors of the report did not give much attention to the exact status of the information they decided to present as statements of fact. This was not a matter of concern to them. It didn't enter their minds, probably. For instance:

Willis was finishing his freshman year at Dunbar when a teenage gang killed him. Gang members met him on the street and shot him in the head at point-blank range.

Unlike the case of Cornell Steele killing James McCain, where the report notes that Steele was found guilty of murder by a court, the report does not elaborate on the identity of the killers of Willis Clayton or the eventual disposition of their cases or whether they are awaiting trial, or have yet to be arrested. In the absence of this essential material or a note explaining that the material exists and cannot be made public, the authors of the report would have been better advised to have written:

Willis was finishing his freshman year at Dunbar when a [n alleged] teenage gang killed him. [Police officers state that alleged] gang members met him in the street. . . .

The question of pretrial rights of any accused assailants is not the point. What is the status of the information? It is, precisely, report of allegation, and should be stated in just that precise way. When such precision is lacking, a reader assumes, from the words he is reading, that the information is fact. It could become fact only because the authors of the report allowed it to climb in quality and certitude from allegation to fact. I count forty-nine instances in the report where the authors convert police-supplied information into the hard reality of historical fact.

Were this ordinary sloppiness one meets in bureaucratic documents, it would be merely irritating. More than sloppiness is involved. The basic doctrines of American jurisprudence have been literally set aside. Is it not the case across the American republic that the only final and finally safe judge of crime is a court of law, whether judge or jury? No matter how spectacular an event, how many eyewitnesses —as was the case when Jack Ruby shot Lee Oswald on television— it is merely an event until a court has pondered the evidence of those many eyewitnesses and considered it in light of the spectacular charge and utters the word "guilty." Only then is it appropriate to speak of a crime having been committed. Short of that deliberative "guilty" there is no real sense to the use of the word "crime." "Organized

Youth Crime in Chicago" regularly presents as crime the written reports of police officers, their suspicions, opinions, judgments, and their reports of the suspicions, opinions, and judgments of others. Consider the following case:

Charles Strong, 17, lived in a neighborhood controlled by the the Blackstone Rangers, but he refused to join the gang. Rangers had beaten him and fired shots into his home, until his family finally moved to a new neighborhood. Word got back to the Rangers that he had joined the Disciples. On May 27, 1969, Strong came back to the neighborhood to see a girl friend. They sat on her porch until 10:30 P.M. when 15 Rangers approached from an alley and ordered them to freeze.

One of the gang fired a shot at his feet and another grabbed his clothes at the back of the neck and ordered him to walk fast. They went into an alley.

He shouted, "Don't kill me." They beat him and he fell. He lay in the alley and did not speak again. One of the gang stood over him with a revolver and carefully pointed the barrel at the back of Charles Strong's head. Methodically, he pulled the trigger four times.

One or two of the gang looked at Strong's body. Blood was coming from holes in the back of his head and at the base of his neck. Then they left.

Eight Rangers were arrested and indicted by the grand jury (p. 15).*

Although a footnote calls the account an account, it is offered as a true account of what happened to Charles Strong. In that act the authors have converted arrest and indictment into certainty of guilt, which they are not able to do unless they set aside the doctrines of jurisprudence which reign across America. Rather than assume the authors maliciously set out to overcome 1,000 years of Anglo-Saxon/American legal experience, I assume they did not think about what they were doing. It didn't occur to them that a grand jury is not a court and that a grand jury merely marks a state's case as cogent enough to go into court with. It didn't occur to them that evidence so compelling within the unchallengeable precincts of a report might not prove as compelling before a court. Why would such doubts arise in minds

*Footnote reads: "The account summarizes police reports, State's Attorney reports and newspaper statements, including *Chicago Today,* May 31, 1969, and *Chicago Daily News,* June 23, 1969."

accustomed to accepting this particular kind of police report on these particular people as true and exactly equivalent to criminal act?

Inasmuch as the police supplied all of the data in the report, it is all the more important to visualize the situation of the people of the city and the people of Blackstone, between which stand the Chicago police who monitor the proceedings of the people of Blackstone and report to the people of the city. This is an unusual situation. The people of the city would not otherwise put up with it. They almost always want to know about what happens and want to judge for themselves. Ordinarily they have a rich assortment of monitors: reporters, friends, fellow workers, cab drivers, participants, neighbors, friends of friends, *and* the police. Remaining curiosity can be satisfied by going over for a personal look. But in this specific situation the police are the only reporters. Other sources of data were not used. (The report quoted extra-police sources in preparing the "history," and at times used newspaper reports—which reported police reports.) Above all, the data themselves are not heard in the report. The police quote gang members on occasion, but the quotations are not words directly spoken from the people of Blackstone to the people of the city. The quotations are derived from words Blackstone speaks to police, to each other, or to parties involved in criminal conflict.

Had the authors of the report interviewed Blackstone on any or all of the areas of the report, Blackstone perhaps would have answered with a swift obscenity. But then, it is not certain. Perhaps they would have confirmed some of the contentions of the report. The people of Chicago will never know from the authors of this report what is going on in the mind of criminal gang members. Their mind is a total obscurity to the reader save for the illuminations offered by gang experts. They say, for instance:

. . . Ranger leadership has frequently used the assassination-style killing to prevent mass defections or to make an example of certain defectors, especially if they join a rival gang.

Such a statement does not content itself with stating what happened, but *why* it happened. First of all, someone must have known the minds of Ranger leaders. Else how could it be known that Ranger leaders did one thing (used assassination-type killings) in order to accomplish another end (prevent mass defections)? This illuminates some pretty dastardly minds at work, all right, but it is not clear which minds are illuminated—which Ranger leaders', or which authors'. Aside from these disquisitions into Ranger motives, one will not find the Ranger mind, any more than he will hear the Ranger voice.

But why should they speak? Why should they have an opportunity to display their thinking to the people of Chicago? Their crime obliterates their standing. Their records of conviction and "collective" imprisonment show how substantial and long-standing their crime has been. But their view of a sundered Chicago has not been obliterated. It seems to be the view of the authors of the report.

Even the position of enlightened tolerance with which the report so hopefully opens comes to odd conclusions about the limits of that tolerance:

In the field of law enforcement, municipal police are basically organized to meet ordinary criminal activity. They are not typically structured to deal with large-scale criminal organization among youth. The policy of the city's law enforcement agencies has been to give young people special protection when they get into trouble with the law. When picked up by police, youngsters are referred to specially trained officers, brought to a special court, turned over, when confinement is necessary, to youth institutions and supervised by a special staff of probation and parole officers when they are released. Their offences are not made a matter of permanent record, and their names are not made public. . . .

Yet

action must be taken when young men deliberately set out to create a structure which threatens the security of others, even in their own homes; which organize for the avowed purpose of controlling a community's youth populations; which employs its structure to obtain revenue illegally; and which attempts to secure immunity for its crimes through intimidation and violence (p. 6–7).

Who will perform the infinitely delicate task of deciding which youth are eligible for special protection and which youth deserve the other kind—"action"? Moreover *when* will the decision be made, at the moment of membership in one of these "structures" or after the "structures" "threaten" or "control" or "attempt"? Will the law determine these matters, or the council of experts convened for the announced purpose of preparing a "battle plan" to implement a "war"? Neither one, it seems. The police will make the decision as to which will receive special protection and which will get action. The limits of tolerance seemingly are the exact boundaries of the regular and the sub-America. What kind of perversity is this? The report ends up agreeing with the Blackstone it has derided, in fact takes up Blackstone's torch in posing, thoughbeit unwittingly, the basic constitutional question, which is, recall, "Are all people born here in this country gonna be real Americans or only the ones suit *you?*"

August 4, 1969, marked the completion of the process. Careful attention to the document shows an eagerness on the part of the City of Chicago to picture the Black P. Stone Nation under a blanket of absolute, unrelieved criminality, which picture is not matched with a corresponding evidence required to prosecute. In some instances successful prosecution was noted. But only in five instances. The statistics of gross crime, gross shootings, shootings in certain areas, shootings in certain time periods, extortion attempts, murders, the ages of victims, the ages of shooters are contradictory within themselves. For all the "gang-relatedness" which gives them apparent coherence, they have more artistic value than empirical validity. One concludes that the conferring of foeship is an important undertaking best left to experts in that sort of thing. One would not necessarily conclude that this process had been going on for thirty-six months. The report reads almost as though it were telling the real story of the Blackstone Rangers for the first time. In reality it was the grand finale to an old story told many times. There was old "jive", too, for the new "jive" to be piled on top of. The old "jive" is equally instructive.

An editorial appeared in the *Chicago American* (July 10, 1968) during the time of the so-called McClellan hearings. It bore a promising title, "U.S. Displeases Jeff Fort" which is certainly true. But the *American* editorial writers didn't quite mean it that way.

The U.S. Government has displeased Jeff Fort and his lawyer, and we guess will have to take the consequences. Fort, a leader of the Blackstone Rangers, and his lawyer stormed out of a Senate subcommittee hearing yesterday and were declared in contempt of Congress. . . . The theory operating here seems to be that Fort, being an underprivileged product of the black ghetto, owes absolutely nothing to the government's laws or institutions and may defy them at will. On the other hand the government, having sinned against Fort by not making life easier for him, owes him instant compliance in anything he (or his lawyer) may ask. The theory is about due for a test and we hope it gets one. If (Marshall) Patner establishes his client's right to defy Congress, Congress will certainly have proved the contempt was justified.

Reading the editorial is like watching a shell game. The pea is under this, that, the other, *which* shell? The pea, of course, is Jeff Fort's standing in the republic. For the purposes of considering him a contemptuous American, he is provided an honorary citizenship. But it is quickly withdrawn. Apparently he doesn't have the right to press for due process and should have submitted to questioning by the Congressional tribunal without the due process he sought, because he does not have the right. This dazzlingly quick giving and retrieving can also be observed in the "theory" which the writers devise as a working explanation of how Jeff Fort's contempt might be explained. This is a "theory" about a "theory." It is the editorial's theory about what Jeff Fort theorizes. As underprivileged, he thinks he owes nothing to the law = he is a criminal; as American as he thinks the law should heed his rights. Well, he can't have it both ways, can he? If he wants protection from the law, he should take his punishment first, untrammeled by considerations of the first, fourth, fifth, and fourteenth amendments, since that was the issue his lawyer unsuccessfully sought to introduce at the hearings. The editorial is quite sure about that. If the Congress lets him get away with the pretense of being protected by these amendments, the Congress "will certainly have proved the contempt was justified."

One may assume from such exhibitions of civic-mindedness that something like a rule exists. The Blackstone Rangers in their mounting negative acclaim will appear as criminals, but citizens nonetheless. When they act as though they were citizens of the community, maybe underprivileged, the rule judges them to be pretending.

A youth worker on the south side told a reporter he had quit trying to work with the Rangers. He was trying to help them and they resisted. So he quit and took a job where he could really help boys who want help. He concludes from his experience, "The Blackstone Rangers are illegitimate, irresponsible, and do not want to change." And, he adds, they are not a "constructive community organization." That appearance is a put-on which cannot be accepted.*

An unrelated pair of articles condemns a far more obnoxious evidence of pretense. In the first article, the ace crime reporter for the *Chicago Daily News* (June 25, 1968), Art Petacque, outlines a plot revealed to him by anonymous official police spokesmen. These sources told him about Jeff Fort's attempt to buy off a police detective. It was a hush-hush spy and counterspy sort of plot. The article ends on an oddly incongruous note. "As leader of the Rangers, Fort drives a new white sports car, although, except for two months when he worked for the Office of Economic Opportunity, he has not been employed for two years." However terrible the effort to compromise an officer of the law, it is next to nothing. Consider, please, Jeff Fort riding around in an automobile. The gall of the fellow seems unlimited; he is riding around in a *white sports car!* And he doesn't even work. Had he only arranged to have a daddy who might have bought him the car, that would, of course, be fine since there are lots of American boys riding around in sports cars who do not work. Failing that, had he worked with his own hands and saved his money and bought the sports car, that, too, would be acceptable. He did neither. So he cannot be allowed to get away with pretending to be a regular American boy.

This identical trend of outrage was made clear by Winston P.

*Chicago American, June 26, 1968.

Moore, warden of the Cook County Jail and never one to hide behind some pussyfooting "official spokesman" label. He wants to be identified as a source of data against Blackstone Rangers. He was a fountainlike source of data. On one occasion he was speaking with his usual directness against Ranger deceit, their put-on, their attempt to make people believe they were poor American boys. He wanted people to know the facts. "Let's face it," he is reported (*Chicago American,* June 21, 1968) to have said, "these gangs have turned into a black Mafia of Chicago, selling dope, prostitution, and engaging in extortion or doing anything for a buck." Moore tells Chicagoans to look beyond this momentary appearance of the Blackstone Rangers as actual Americans who might really have a chance to get work and settle down. It is a mischievous appearance at best. They are not trying to work. They are working a cheap hustle, a pay-off racket, getting a Job Training Project for the kickbacks it provides the Ranger treasury. And he thinks he knows what that money is used for: "to buy guns and probably cars. All the leaders have cars even though they do not have jobs" *(ibid).*

Since Moore had just taken it upon himself to speak for the entire "Negro Community," including "the militants," he wanted it to be known that he was upset, the people whom he represented were upset at the sight of these leaders driving around in *cars.* Who, indeed, do they think they are? A veritable Thorstein Veblen is required to reveal the complexities of *this* conspicuous riding in cars though out of work. A Jean-Paul Sartre is needed to examine the whirligigs of pretense the Rangers are working on Chicago, the little, how-do-you-call-it?, fakes. But, of course! That is precisely what they are: FAKE AMERICANS.

What is the substance of their pretense? It is twofold. They are pretending not to be criminals. That seems to be the uppermost theme. But, they are also pretending to be regular Americans, and that too seems to be the uppermost theme. They are both uppermost, of course, because together they comprise the essence of pretense.

At all costs the Blackstone Rangers cannot be allowed direct participation in Chicago public experience as actual citizens. The doctrine of pretense stops any efforts they might make. In order to participate in this experience—or in the marginal areas of public debate—they should first cleanse themselves of the criminality. Since it exists as a charge-message, and they are not the ones initiating it, how exactly might they go about cleansing themselves, except by debating the particulars of the charge-message, which they cannot do until they are cleansed? The lines of a double bind emerge. They are prohibited from saying what is required as a prerequisite for having something to say worth listening to. R.D. Laing's marvelously comprehensive theorem comes to mind once more: "The greater need there is to get out of an intolerable position the less chance there is of doing so. The more untenable a position is, the more difficult it is to get out of it."

Crime is no longer what a judge determines criminals do, or what policemen report that criminals do; crime has become a state of the criminal's mind; crime is a propensity toward crime. Crime inheres in the gang member as his essence. Wherever he goes, crime goes with him. Whomever he meets is infected. He is a virus set loose to plague the city. By all means, action must be taken to prohibit contact between the virus-carriers and the uncontaminated. The police, with such a vision, cannot be faulted for striving to preserve the precious difference between the sick and the healthy by quarantining the plague area.

To the mayor, appropriately enough, goes the honor of having the last word.

The concern of the city of Chicago is to make every neighborhood a safe place in which to live, a community where children may go to schools, playgrounds and parks without danger of attack, where adults may shop, attend church and meetings and visit friends without fear, and where businesses may be conducted without intimidation. Residents of our communities at times are not permitted to enjoy the freedom of movement without fear of attack because of the conduct of individuals banded together for criminal purposes who prey upon the residents of neighborhoods. These criminal gangs extort money from businessmen and also from school children. They burglarize, assault, rob, rape, and murder. By their action they seek to terrorize the community for the sole purpose of personal enrichment. Their actions indicate that they have no regard for their community or its residents, but are interested only in their personal gain. . . . They seek to cloak this criminal activity under the guise of social involvement and what they advertise as constructive endeavors. Unfortunately, some groups which have no real knowledge of the community disregard the record and are misled into supporting criminally led gangs.*

All of Chicago lies before him—industrious, churchgoing, visiting friends and family on Sunday afternoons, the children happily at play. Is this not the clue to what he is saying? Where are the Stone peoples in the mayor's Chicago? Where are the broken, distracted, hungry, assaulted, addicted people whose heads are full of rage at the insult life has been to them since birth? They are not in the mayor's Chicago. They have been banished from recognition. So they are the not-theres, the not-visiting friends and family on Sunday afternoons, the not-industrious, the not-church going. But this not-existence is not a total obscurity. It turns out they *are* there in their null shape. Almost melodramatically they reveal themselves to be there right along: as Chicago's ravagers and enemies.

To the subpoverty of Stones and Stone peoples has been added a war and a hatred. Chicago cannot endure part free and part criminal —by its own multiple admissions. Give or take the word "criminal," that would be Blackstone's view, too.

*Chicago Sun-Times, July 20, 1969.

5   A Criminal Church

Sure they can play a role. In the case of the churches, I think it would be along the lines of religious orientation—teaching right from wrong, the Golden Rule concept. It just does not seem to me the role of the church is advocating revolution or hostility against the establishment.

Edward Buckney, in the *Chicago Sun Times,* July 29, 1969

I have mentioned that Blackstone was not without friends and supporters during the time the hated metamorphosis was occurring. I was among those friends and supporters in my capacity as an outraged American citizen and more prominently as pastor of the First Presbyterian Church of Chicago which is located in Woodlawn, squarely in the Stone territory. The official board of the church, called a Session, officially sanctioned a program of relationship with the Blackstone Rangers in February, 1966, and began to employ a staff to carry out the program.

The session and the 560 member congregation of the church began the program with one end in mind: to curtail rampant violence in Woodlawn. Church officials and the "Ranger Staff" saw that saying to Blackstone, "Violence is wrong and must be stopped" would be fruitless since Blackstone already knew that. We entered on another course. We sought to provide actual alternatives to violence in the form of expanded life possibilities for individual Rangers and for the organization itself. As it came to know Blackstone at first hand, the staff came to see—in the most ambivalent and unclarified mode, I recall—that violence and criminality were not equivalent terms. It led the church into open contest with the official City of Chicago and particularly its police department.

The church had little understanding of what it was doing in the opening months of the Ranger program. The director of the staff, Charles Lapaglia, knew what he was doing but the church was full of the vague self-righteousness which flows through the veins of people who are doing good. It was a downright pleasure for the people of the congregation to know that something was being done. The Rangers were messy, church members knew, and they smoked cigarettes inside the richly appointed sanctuary of the church building, but they were *inside* the church.

There was a confluence between what the people of First Church thought a church—any church—*should* be doing and what they were actually doing.

Concerning the grave assertions Blackstone was making about American society, church members ordinarily knew nothing. Their idea was justice. This was the word they summoned to describe the goal in mind. During that summer I encountered a policeman beating a boy on 63rd Street and in anger interposed myself between them, daring the policeman to beat me up before he further abused the child. The civil liberatarian wing of the church membership took that to be symbolic of the Ranger program. The church would interpose itself between police and Blackstone and dare the police to beat the church up before it continued abusing Blackstone. In drawing the hasty correlations, these people did not attend to the possible different consequences of interposition, the most outstanding of which was that the police, if dared, might do it, might wade in, beat the church up, then proceed with its beating up of Blackstone.

Justice awaited doing. Here were some of the poor, abused, hungry, ill-clothed, ill-housed, run-over little people whom the very Lord Jesus had commanded First Church to stand with and to serve. Getting justice for them was understood to be the program. Instances of injustice kept intervening, however. The police were arresting Rangers in large numbers as summer approached, on what the church understood to be flimsy if not illegal grounds. This was holding up the doing of good. We were not getting on with the business of curtailing violence, because, as the church saw the matter, the police were pumping up the violence. The church responded by contesting these mass arrests with mass bail bonds.

Church members came to see at first hand that the major obstacle to achieving success in its program was the police. There was full agreement on this view. A vivid animus against the police began to develop. This exploded into active hatred following the celebrated raid on First Church in November, 1966 (see Appendix). As a consequence, the church was ready to do battle with the police on account of the wrong it had suffered, including a readiness to do battle on the issue of this Blackstone criminality the police were forever talking about.

I cannot fairly say that First Church was aware of the audacious Blackstone assertions; they condemned the church no less than the other institutions of regular America. I cannot change history in order to present First Church as a participant in the creation of a summons to America. It remained for Blackstone to teach the church about the actual structures of injustice, and to encourage the church to seek the truth; this evangelical education of the church proceeded slowly. In its first stages, the program called for Church to teach Stone how to shut down violence. Accordingly the church entered the battle with the police on the side of simple constitutional justice and fought the battle as skillfully and fiercely as it knew how to do. With our simple view of a single America, we understood ourselves to be championing the rights of the poorest of all. Whether or not we were as much enemy of Blackstone as the police, thus, needs pondering.

The police saw First Church's program with Blackstone, its willingness to defend Blackstone, as a direct interference. The police were perplexed, possibly, by the combination of straight church and hoodlum gang, but direct anger overtook any perplexity. In expressing this anger the police began to apply the same procedures to the church they were applying to Blackstone, among which was an attempt to impute criminality to the church. The church got sucked up into the general metamorphosis, and began learning at first hand how it feels to be converted into criminals by the mere words of police officers. To self-righteousness about our cause was added knowledge of our innocence of the charges being hurled at us. These marvelously good people, rich and poor, black and white, old and young, *knew* in their lived experience as individuals and as a church that they were not criminals and then felt the utter frustration of having always to be proving what they were *not* before asserting what they were.

The major episode in the metamorphosis of First Church from a justice-seeking to a crime-doing church occurred in June-July 1968, during the McClellan Committee hearings. It would be bootless to pretend, against the widely known facts of history, that I was merely one or an incidental figure in those hearings. And it would be dishonest to tell that story in anything less than actual first-person terms. But in employing first-person narrative, I do not forswear my interests, which are, recall, directed toward the eventual excavation of the primary issue. What happened to me is a necessary detour the police and I took from the main issue.

The Reverend Goes to Washington

According to a sometimes reliable Evans and Novak column syndicated July 8, 1968, the famous McClellan Subcommittee on Investigations, operating under the Senate Committee on Government Operations hearings on the T.W.O. Job Training Project were proposed by detectives of the Gang Intelligence Unit of the Chicago Police Department. Evans and Novak report that field investigators for the McClellan Committee came to Chicago following the west side disorders in January, 1968. They couldn't find much to investigate. G.I.U. detectives asked them to "look at this juicy stuff," and pulled out their files on the Blackstone Rangers, First Church, and T.W.O.

The investigators agreed it was promising. In fact, it was sensational. It was exactly what the senator needed to get back into national prominence.

My going to Washington began on Friday morning, June 21. Lois Wille (a *Chicago Daily News* reporter) phoned me about ten o'clock and said, "Hey, dad, do you know what George Rose is saying about you in Washington?"

Her jocularity miscued me. I joked along.

"He has just testified that you passed along a murder command from Gene Hairston to kill Robert Straughter." End of jokes. The breezy opening was her way of saying she didn't believe it. Did I want to say something for the record? Yes, I did.

"If George Rose would take a lie detector test on that testimony he would blow the fuses out of the machine." I added a categorical denial.

The phone rang again. It was Leon Finney, Executive Director of T.W.O.

"You heard what's goin' down in Washington?"

"Only about the murder command."

"Shit. He's said a *whole lot* of stuff. We're having a press conference right away in the Project office. See you there and we can talk."

Before I could get out of my chair the phone rang a third time. It was Jerome Adlerman, chief counsel for the McClellan Committee. Would Monday be convenient for me to appear before the committee as a witness? You bet it would.

Then off I went to the press conference in order to establish some things about George "Watusi, MadDog" Rose.

"George Rose once was a respected and valuable member of the Black P. Stone Nation. He was kicked out of the Nation last September for violation of its policy against the use of narcotics. Last January he was involved, apparently, in a bungled hand-off of something like a quarter of a million dollars' worth of marijuana. He was arrested. But the charges have since been lifted. He is now cooperating with the Gang Intelligence Unit of the Chicago Police Department. If Alighieri Dante can be believed, George Rose will one day find himself in the lowest circle of hell, reserved especially for traitors."

"Reverend Fry, do you think George Rose would be safe coming back to Woodlawn?"

"If you are asking, do I think the Stones would retaliate, the answer is No. They wouldn't have to do anything but look at him. George Rose would die of shame."

Lots of Stones had come over to the church as the news of Watusi's performance began to percolate through Woodlawn. Chuck Lapaglia and his staff associate, Ann Schwalbach, were in the office talking to the Stones when I returned. The Stones went out of their way to give me the benefit of their wisdom on the matter.

"Tusi's a chump, Fry. He fox hisself. You watch." That was good news and about as irrelevant as the "Be cools" they were uttering. Now I was in the Stone place. They enjoyed seeing me relate to the experience. Behind the amusement was more than idle curiousity. They were concerned. I might break under the strain and go all the way over to the police. What else would they expect of a white guy?

We had to find a lawyer. Chuck had been worrying about a lawyer for *Jeff* until that Friday. Mr. Adlerman had just invited Chuck to Washington. A lawyer was needed for Jeff, me, and now Chuck. Our politics dictated Leo Holt. He was a terrific man. He was tough on the basic issues. Moreover, he had done legal work for us and had distinguished himself as a better-than-average lawyer. He had consented to represent Jeff already. But he was planning for a date in the neighborhood of July 10. Would he accept two new clients.

"I've got a jury trial going on."

"We can't go bareback."

"No way. I've got a jury in the box."

That was a setback. We had to move on. But to whom? None of us believed that either Chuck or I would be the crucial figure. We agreed completely, without even talking about it, that Jeff was the star figure. He was the one they were after. We deferred to Jeff. Jeff wanted the Bull. Ann phoned the Bull. He would be right over. Jeff phoned the poolhall and told any Mains there to come over right away. Soon we all sat down to talk about this delicate matter.

Chuck opened up by drawing the big picture: what the Senate is;

who McClellan is; what Watusi had said; the city's politics in busting the Project; G.I.U.'s attempt to bust First Church with bad publicity. Then he put the issue. Should we go for a black lawyer as a matter of principle or should we try to get a Ross, Hardies lawyer and open up a possibility for a Stone law firm which until that day looked like months away? (Preliminary conversations had already taken place between Charles Kettering II, First Church representatives, and the law firm, Ross, Hardies, O'Keefe, Babcock, McDugald, & Parsons. These conversations centered in the possibility of retaining the firm to provide a special legal-defense team for clients known by First Church to be in particular need of legal defense, notably Stones. Charles Kettering had previously supported special defense efforts undertaken in behalf of various Stone leaders. He had expressed interest in supporting a more far-reaching and comprehensive effort.)

Five hours later the meeting ended. It was a bitter meeting during which First Church and Blackstone hammered out a fundamental accord on beginning a legal-defense project. The way was then clear to contact Bill Brackett, the attorney of the Ross, Hardies firm who would head up the projected Stone defense unit. He was in Ann Arbor, Michigan, attending an A.C.L.U. conference. He said he knew very little about what had happened in Washington that day. He would make some calls, he assured us, then let us know his answer.

Bill Brackett in Ann Arbor phoned his firm's associates in Washington; Lloyd, Cutler, and his associates in Chicago; and Jerome Adlerman at his home in Georgetown. Bill then called us back. He had found out some things and, yes, he would be our counsel on Monday. Our gratification was instantly modified by the things he had found out:

—We were in serious trouble.

—If I was going to be able to read a statement into the record of the proceedings—and it would be my only chance to say fully, without interruption and badgering, what I wanted to say—the statement had to be in Mr. Adlerman's hands by 10:30 Sunday morning, twenty-four hours before my appearance, by committee rule.

—I must stay away from any more statements to the press.

—He was cutting the conference and would be at First Church by one o'clock Saturday afternoon.

Saturday was a twenty-hour-long blur of confusion. The statement was prepared. A testimonial brigade of celebrated national and south side personages was lined up who said the John Fry they knew would not pass along murder commands. During the afternoon Mike Royko called.

He proposed I meet him on Sunday morning at nine. We would go to an outfit which does polygraph tests. I would take a full polygraph test on the Rose allegations. Then, promised Royko, he would "blow the clown [McClellan] out of the water." I accepted right off. But Bill and Chuck were upset. They didn't suspect Royko of funny business. They suspected the firm. Chuck knew the firm. Bill knew the firm even better. This was the firm the police used. Royko had said he thought he could guarantee the objectivity of the test. That was good enough for me. Mike Royko is one of my heroes. At the moment I can't think of anyone else I would rank as a literal hero, so I had better change it to a singular hero. I think he is one of the few great men around these days. If he would guarantee the test, I felt safe. I was eager to take the test. Two things were going on. I wanted to display my innocence. But also, it was a great trick to play. It was part of a politics of resistance. It fitted like a glove with my first remark to Lois Wille on Friday. I would lead the way in taking a lie detector test. Mike Royko wanted to help out! Couldn't they see that?

Yes, they could see it, but they were still against the idea. They argued, "Even Mike Royko cannot guarantee the test. As soon as he calls up to make the appointment, they will phone the cops. You gotta *know* that will happen. You know there will be funny business in the test. The test will be bad. This is Daley's town, not Royko's. Royko wouldn't print the test was bad. For him it would be only the loss of some hot copy. But the *Tribune* would print the test was bad in headlines bigger than the end of the war. John, you *know* that is the only way it could go." They were urgent and sweating. They were in it with me. What are counselors for? Against my better judgment, I agreed to call it off. "But,"—to Bill—"you call it off with Royko. I haven't the heart."

Sunday was not a blur. Ann took the first plane from O'Hare to Washington, Bill took the next plane. As Chuck and I were preparing to leave, Jeff Fort made a special point in order to focus our understanding on the week ahead; he said, "Senate ain't shit." Immediately we remembered the scrawled signs all over Woodlawn which announced, "D's ain't shit," and, in spite of our anxiety, we had to laugh at his grim truth. The Senate really ain't shit. We caught the noon plane and went directly to the offices of Lloyd, Cutler, there to confer with Bill and an attorney named Dan Mayer, associated with the firm and a specialist on the subject of congressional hearings. We discovered that Bill Brackett was a specialist, too. He had represented natural-gas firms in numerous rate hearings before congressional committees. The two of them knew what they were doing.

Dan Mayer had spent Saturday in the offices of the McClellan Committee reading the transcript of George Rose's testimony. He and Bill had been determining the actual allegations to worry about. They had almost completed the job. The murder command allegation might conceivably involve me in criminal action as a conspirator. It was barely possible. Aside from that, Rose hadn't alleged I had done anything actually criminal. The lawyers said, "If everything he said about you were true, people might find you crazy, but a state's attorney couldn't prosecute."

They couldn't determine Chuck's freedom from possible criminal culpability as surely because Rose had testified that Chuck had carried guns from Michigan to Illinois in his car, and, were that true, he possibly would have violated a federal law governing the transport of firearms across state lines. It was a matter they were researching when we arrived.

The main order of business was going to be criminal stuff. The lawyers wanted to discover as much as they could from our own lips what had really happened. They wanted to know from us—not George Rose—the literal, complete story. A faint catch-22 flavor was necessarily mixed into the conference. "When didn't you pass along murder commands?" "I always didn't pass along murder commands." The lawyers wanted to satisfy themselves on these points: Had we done anything criminal? Had we seen anything criminal? Had we taken part, passively, in anything criminal, meaning, did we allow it to happen when vigorous action might have stopped it?

Naturally the lawyers wanted precise but full answers. We didn't have any of those. Chuck is the greatest avoider of a conclusion or the end of a story I have ever known. He circles around a point like a gull in a windstorm. And I have to explain two or three preliminary items before I can tell you what time it is. The lawyers got full answers, all right, but hardly precise answers. Furthermore, Chuck and I tend to try to convert new hearers of the great old stories of Blackstone and First Church. Furthermore, we were annoyed that the lawyers could harbor the merest theoretical suspicion we had anything to hide. Consequently the conference often resembled a tug-of-war. Were there any Fifth-Amendment-type materials, they wanted to know. They wanted to find out there in the privacy of the office, not before national television. We were not interested in that. We were trying to get the lawyers wise enough to the street, to the issues—to *Chicago* —to understand word one of what we had to tell them. We began with Moses, moved carefully through John the Baptist, Malcolm X, and James Brown, to set the stage for arriving at the poolhall on 67th Street where Chuck was looking for Jeff.

The conference was not antagonistic. It was a hurry-up period of getting acquainted. The lawyers had laid it down this way:

"One section of the public is already disposed to believe George Rose. You must not give these people another reason to believe him.

"Another section of the public is now disposed to disbelieve George Rose. You must not provide these people a good reason to take back the benefit of the doubt they have extended to you. An incident will turn them against you.

"The Senators themselves don't care about you. They care about the politics of killing O.E.O. They want publicity. But they will begin caring about you if you provoke them. They will, in fact, want to cut you into little pieces. You are the occasion for the committee to reach the living rooms of America."

This bleak analysis was confirmed later that evening by Phil Newell, a long-time trusted friend. He was representing the not inconsiderable interests of the United Presbyterian Church in the U.S.A. And he is a charter member of the Washington inside-scoop club. One of his staff people had been snooping around. Phil had been thinking about the matter all weekend. His advice was more somber than the lawyers'.

"You are dead, no matter what you do. If you are very good, and I mean, if you are positively brilliant, you will not drag the whole C.A.P. (Community Action Program) component of O.E.O. down with you. You are going to go down. Your goal is negative. Your goal is not to have headlines saying you fight with Senator John. You can be a fiery-eyed fool to benefit your own soul, or you can continue to do something for people. Judas-goat or sacrificial lamb? Which?"

According to real politics you do not in ecstasy make up your way, as though inspired and, with a mighty "Black . . . STONE!" charge. You settle down. You plot out every possible thing that can happen and plan what you are going to do. That's what we did at the conference. We developed our overall strategy, based on our predictions of what was going to happen. The strategy was defensive. It was centered in my appearance on the stand. All four of us, and later Phil Newell, had a hand in devising it.

"John Fry, you will present yourself on the witness stand in such a way as to give every indication that the allegations against you couldn't be true. Your primary audience is the stenographer making a record of the proceedings. Pretend that there are semihostile citizens listening intently to your every word. You will want to convince them with everything you say and by your general demeanor that the charges against you are ridiculous, because you are, with your demeanor, disproving them."

The rules for appearing before the committee were repeated for me by the lawyers as though chiseled in stone directly after Moses had completed the Tenth Commandment. The rules were an amalgam of experience and apprehension.

1. There is inadvertent perjury which is technically not as bad as real perjury, but it is perjury nonetheless. Stay out of it. The senators will attempt to trap you into inadvertent perjury. They will do this

by suddenly switching from subject to subject. The chairman is a past master at this form of questioning. He will want to rattle you into a mistake. Once you have made a mistake he will hope to get real perjury, where you have lied on purpose in order to cover up something you in your rattled state think might be damaging. If you commit inadvertent perjury, admit it immediately, and suffer the insinuations. Penitence beats bravado.

2. If you see a perjury-type issue looming, don't answer the question. Talk to Bill Brackett. Explain the problem to him, then take his advice. He is better prepared than you will be to make those decisions. The senators will try to make something sinister out of your turning to your counsel. Don't let them bluff you. It is your right to seek counsel before you answer any question.

3. Build a record of politeness. You needn't be obsequious about it. Call the senators "Sir" and the chairman, "Mr. Chairman." They are not your pals. If you find yourself just once saying, in a dangerously intimate tone, "Senator Curtis" or "Senator Mundt" (they'll be the only senators from the committee on hand, probably), you have gone into their coziness trap. Resist it. Imagine they are poisonous snakes. You can respect what they will do to you best by not getting friendly with them. They are *not* your friends.

4. Answer the questions they ask and only the questions they ask. Don't get wrapped up in the subject and blab on and on. That probably won't be a problem. You will probably not be able to finish an answer before you are interrupted. Let them interrupt. Pay attention to the questions and answer them. If the senators don't want to hear all of the answer, that's not your affair. You will have tried, and the record will show it.

5. Don't blow up. You will have good enough amplification so you won't have to speak in louder than a conversational tone. If you catch yourself speaking more loudly than that, you are in bad trouble. Stop. Don't say another word; ask for a recess; you have to go to the bathroom; light up a cigarette; talk to Bill Brackett. Do anything until you are assured you are back down to that conversational level of volume. For your protection, Bill will be listening for a volume change

you may not realize. If he hears it, he is prepared with legal maneuvers or will think of something to break you off before you commit suicide.

6. Don't swear. You swear more than too much. Clergymen don't swear at all, ever. You are a clergyman. A badge can be prepared for you to wear on your lapel, as a reminder, saying, "This man is a clergyman." If a swear word comes in a direct quote of something you are answering truthfully, don't say it. Spell it or paraphrase it, and tell the senators you are paraphrasing. Along the same line, don't use hip talk. Use regular English.

7. Don't try to win. Try to be alive when it is over. That is what winning means for you. There is no way you can win in your own terms. It is rigged the other way. If you are still breathing and not in jail when you are dismissed, that is victory.

Monday and the hearings arrived. You might have suspected, with obvious reason, when I listed the rules for appearing before the McClellan Committee, that I made them up after the fact as a distillation of what I learned during my appearances. I make a point of this because I want you to know I really did have those rules drummed into me before the hearings began. I had the benefit of experienced counsel. I knew the rules before I got there. After a few minutes in the chair my appreciation of Bill Brackett, Dan Mayer, and Phil Newell soared. They had done their homework well. I didn't like what was happening, but it wasn't taking me by surprise.

Each time I think about the actual sessions I dismiss the run of questions and answers as unworthy of further thought. Call it intellectual vanity. I was that far ahead of the lead-minded senators. But examine the presupposition of my disinterest in the literal questions and answers. I did actually have clean hands. I could have passed an honest lie-detector test without an instant's worry. Regardless of the reigning presumption of my undoubted guilt because of the mere volume of spectacular allegation, I was clean. I had no need for brilliant maneuvers to stay out of bad holes, or for clever dissimulation to protect myself, or staff, or Stones. Let that presupposition resonate a bit. The senators asked me point-blank, "Didn't you for a fact know . . . such-and-such . . . some murder-pot-sex-guns-violence-extortion?" I had already made a categorical denial and named it categorical. Interest in the literal minute-by-minute proceedings would be juiced up appreciably if now I could furnish a "what really happened" memorandum to go with the transcript. To move through the endless inanities of what I didn't do, what I didn't know, is remotely foolish. The hearings were, in one word, tedious.

It was my word against someone else's word. The senators went positively out of their way to rephrase my answers in such a way as to make them sound unbelievable. The general strategy and the rules for appearance forbade me messing around with their questions, even when they were garbled versions of answers I had just given. My department was answers. Their department was questions. Throughout I judged the quality of the questions to be poor, even within the context of their strategy. They weren't interested in information I had. I couldn't turn their questions into good questions. So I endured to the end, concentrating on doing my job. Like a defensive tackle in a football game. Your team may be getting beaten 38–0 in the first quarter, but if you have any pride in your job, you attend to each play, you pick up your keys, you protect your zone, you try to beat the man in front of you. So the content of the questions was the same old predictable murder, pot, sex, violence, extortion. What did I know about it? Nothing. But you must know something about it. The Blackstone Rangers do it and you are their spiritual adviser. No, I am not. What are you? Their friend. They met in your church? Yes. Didn't you give them the benefit of spiritual advice. No. What kind of advice did you give them? Legal advice. Didn't you ever pray with them? No. They met in your church. Right. So you knew about it, since they did it in your church. No. And so on. Careful. Tedious. Unbelievable. It was doubly unbelievable to me that the thing was even happening. It was unbelievable to the senators that you can put First Presbyterian Church and Blackstone into the same moral universe.

It became apparent that I was a calloused liar or a sucker. I let it be that decision: liar or sucker. They could not get me to admit, plainly or by an inadvertency, that I knew about the evil so freely alleged to have happened in the church. Look at it from their chairs.

If they were to admit to themselves for an instant that I was actually telling the truth, they would have to conclude they had been badly used by the Chicago Police Department, and to begin preparing contempt citations against the whole bunch. It couldn't all *not* be true, or else the hearings were over. Therefore, I said I didn't know about it = I was stupid.

Alongside the mounting possibility of my stupidity, and in order to strengthen it, the senators repeatedly sought to drive me into culs-de-sac. Either the Stones are treacherous criminals or angels. Either they are an incipient black Mafia or a constructive community organization. That's easy. I didn't go into the trap. I stayed out. I kept saying one thing, the truth. These are ghetto kids who have put together their own organization. It is a community organization of the youth. In spite of my plain answers, the senators proceeded onward as though I were maintaining that the Stones are a nice, violence-free, Boy Scout troop. The background to the senators' left was filled with enormous displays of the pictures of the Main Twenty-One with their names underneath, big statistical graphs, and a rundown on the criminal record of everyone on the billboard-sized chart. This was the Boy Scout troop I was maintaining the Blackstone Rangers were. I didn't yield. Let them say I said it fifty times, but I didn't say it. *They* said I said it.

Bill Brackett served me well. He did his homework well. He gave me expert advice as the hearings ran on. That was his job. It was not his job to become furious. It was not his job to work the night through preparing *his* statement to be read into the record. Admiration turned to wonder when I discovered he was going to make a statement of his own. He had become appalled and then revolted by the thing going on in front of him. He prepared a statement not because he was a lawyer or a good lawyer or a great lawyer (which he is). He prepared a statement of his patriotic outrage over the Chicago Police dominated proceedings of a senatorial tribunal.

The Tuesday afternoon session was called off. The senators had to be on the floor of the Senate. A young man accidentally fell in with a part of the Chicago Police Department group which was at the hearings. He went to lunch with them. He had some questions he wanted to ask them. The young man heard their glee at how well things were going and he also heard "That sonofabitch will die when she gets on the stand." This young man knew someone who knew someone who knew Phil Newell. Obviously it was an important piece of information. Phil worked his inside-scoop machine all afternoon but it wouldn't produce the name of the mysterious "she." The more the young man was put under pressure, the more he seemed to remember that he might have heard wrong and heard "he" instead of "she."

We did our best to plan ahead for the mysterious witness coming up. Even when we were thinking exclusive "she" possibilities, the one name which we didn't think of was Annabelle Martin. Our intelligence had overflown such an obvious possibility. "You people can't think dirty enough," Bill Brackett said, once we were back in Chicago. We knew Annabelle Martin, all right.

She had been the recipient of emergency help from First Church for three years. We had fed, clothed, and bathed her children. We had furnished her apartment after a fire. Her children had gone to our school. We had helped her in a hundred ways. We knew her—and her history.

Her sons, Sanders and Marvin, used to be Rangers until they got charged with murder. After that, they went over to the police as state's witnesses against Gene Hairston. The charges were dropped, but they can be reinstated at any time. Meanwhile, Annabelle has been taken under "protective custody" and enjoys the good life in the best hotels with food, drink, transportation, and gifts.

We knew that Annabelle was formidable. I have thought that she would make a great spy. She has precisely the skill necessary to function in double- and triple-agent situations. For instance: After she was under protective custody and staying in a posh motel, she phoned one of our teachers. She was being monitored by the police and had just managed to get away for a minute, but she wanted to talk; would the teacher meet her at such-and-such? The teacher went right over. They met. Annabelle wanted to let us know that she knew that a particular Stone wasn't guilty of murder. Another one was guilty. But she didn't dare blow her cover. She would testify who it really was when the trial came up if we (First Church) would get her out of town. The teacher knew enough to know she couldn't negotiate such a business as that. She urged Annabelle to get in touch with Chuck. As they were talking, a member of the G.I.U. stepped out from behind a curtain. The teacher left and contacted Chuck. Chuck stayed with the teacher in anticipation of another call from Annabelle. It came. Annabelle explained to Chuck that she was on our side. Were we to get the money together, she promised to testify. Chuck promised nothing. He invited her to escape the police and come over to make a deposition. *Then* we could talk about going out of town. "By the way," asked Chuck, "why did you spill such vital information before the cop behind the curtain?" "Oh, the G.I.U. knows it," Annabelle said.

Boxes, within boxes, within boxes. We had never been sure where Annabelle stood on anything before—but there was no doubt now. I was flabbergasted when she walked out of the back room and toward the witness chair. She was . . . perfect. The questioning so far had not been successful in breaking me down into pieces and stomping on me. That ideological matter of making me out as a simple dupe was not the way of the Chicago Police Department. They wanted me branded absolutely and forever as a criminal. Annabelle could do it if anyone in the world could. So the reverend says he didn't know about murder and guns and pot and sex and violence and extortion, huh? Well, he did too know and do crime, and this fine ghetto lady, here, is going to tell you all about it.

She did. She had me hauling ammunition, rolling reefers, arranging honeymoon trysts in the church building, being in big drunken brawls in the church building, threatening lawyers, threatening witnesses, terrorizing Woodlawn, getting rich, and just a whole lot more. Her sons had been in that evil Blackstone thing, so she knew all about it. But she saw the light and now she's out of it. She knows what it is to be poor. She knows what it is to struggle. Annabelle has a nonstop way of talking, which, when rendered without pauses between subjects, provides the impression that it is all so genuine she doesn't have to think about it. Well, this is an old ghetto game which senators from Arkansas, North Dakota, and Nebraska have never heard of. They hear someone talking non-stop and they think the truth is spurting out all over them.

I was still the main witness. She had been brought out to sit to my —and Bill's—right. She was sitting no more than a yard and a half away. That made it possible for broad dramatic gestures. "And this *good* Reverend Fry, he . . . " sweeping her arm contemptuously toward me. That was enough. It made little difference what came after the "he," it was true. From the standpoint of the law, her testimony was unfixed in time or space, uncorroborated, and undifferentiated into evidence, hearsay, rumor, and gossip. From the standpoint of the hearing, it was superb. She took away the sucker possibility. I could not be a mere dupe. I was too malevolent. She turned the corner from allegation of knowledge of crime in the church building into doing crime, in fact, master-minding crime. So by the time she had finished I was Fagin.

Eventually the Wednesday morning session closed. We did the only thing we could do. There was no way to repair the damage. The damage had been done in the area of direct sensation. Spectators, press, and senators alike had felt Annabelle's sincerity. They had thrilled to her courage. They had laughed at her humor. (I noticed John Walsh, one of the committee's investigating staff, laughing so hard he had to find a handkerchief to dry his eyes.) There was no way we could snake back through sensations and relocate the impression they had made. We could only retreat to rule number 7: "Don't try to win. Try to be alive when it is over." I denied everything head-on. The committee staff had monitored our press conference at noon. Questions on Wednesday afternoon had, accordingly, been prepared to get me to fight with the senators about their rules. But I didn't. I tried to maintain myself so that there would still be room for people to wonder to themselves whether I might be a little maligned and Annabelle perhaps too eager to do me in.

Lo, how the mighty have fallen. From a position of near invincibil-

ity to this bare possibility that I might *not* be the worst criminal of
this Blackstone bunch, in three days. I am sticking to the facts now.
They are unadorned with fantastic hopes, with maybes, with "if we
do this, that good thing will happen." We were clobbered. Stomped.
Mashed. Ruined. We *got trashed* by the Weatherman wing of the
G.I.U.

According to real politics, we had one basic way on which to go
after the hearings were over. We had to persuade people to believe the
hearings were unfair, that the allegations made in Washington against
First Church and its staff were untrue, and that we were victims of
an immense police conspiracy to do us in. The truth is on our side.
The truth will prevail!!!!! Add five more exclamation points, if need be,
in order to emphasize what a slaphappy statement it is, and how laden
with turgid hope. But it was the only way we had to go. Were we to
churn up some new resistance stuff, we would no longer enjoy the
advantage of being above suspicion. In fact, we would get thrown
square into jail without a second's hesitation on the part of the police.
So all of that tricky stuff, that great resistance razzle-dazzle was ruled
out. We were stuck with the mere truth.

By September, 1968, we had successfully petitioned the Presbytery of Chicago to establish a special committee to investigate the
charges made at Washington against First Church. If the charges
were found to have substance, we would accept the consequences
of censure and possible action in the criminal courts. But if the
charges were found to have no substance, we would have been
vindicated of wrongdoing. Naturally we wanted public hearings,
convened by a panel of nationally respected heavyweights. We
wanted those witnesses who appeared under McClellan's friendly
coaching to face cross-examination. We wanted the world to see
what a *real* investigation would produce. Naturally we didn't get
it. Instead we got secret hearings held by a special committee of
heavyweight Chicago Presbyterians. That was better than nothing,
but not much. The witnesses adverse to First Church in Washington had no reason to submit to questioning by Presbyterians and
to cross-examination by Bill Brackett. The committee, we felt,

would hear First Church witnesses, then would hear that policemen and their witnesses wouldn't testify.

The transcript of the investigation itself ran 2,000 typed pages. That
furnishes an idea of the committee's determination to hear everything.
By its own statement, the committee spent an equal amount of time
discussing the materials of the investigation (eventually 2,000 pages
in length). The committee did a job. It bent over backward to avoid
the appearance of whitewashing First Church. Contrary to its own
agreements and against our will, it had offered to meet adverse witnesses without First Church or Bill Brackett in attendance. It had
made use of established contacts between prestigious Presbyterians
and Chicago officialdom to *force* the appearance of adverse witnesses.
After that effort failed, what other conclusion could the committee
come to? It had to agree with our initial estimates: The witnesses
wouldn't come because if they did come, they would no longer have
the privilege of Congressional immunity.

In September, 1969, fifteen months after the Washington hearings,
the committee reported to Presbytery it could find no wrong in First
Church. The report of this news made page three of the newspapers.
It was the truth, all right, and, sure, the truth will prevail, but—yawn
—so what?

Over my years as a pastor there have been perhaps a dozen people
who came to see me about some fabulous wrong done them in the
courts. They had all the papers in some old bag or a cheap attaché
case: the writs, the motions, the subpeonas. Each paper looked as
though it had been handled hundreds of times. These people had been
done in by some monstrous miscarriage of justice ten or twenty-seven
years before—a long time ago. They were trying to enlist my support
for a fresh attempt at vindication. They were pathetic. The shock of
recognition! *They* were pathetic. Who do you think you are, old man?
How do you escape the same fix, with your papers, your notes, your
manuscripts? Of course. It would appear the bastards did me in, all
right, a long time ago. No doubt about that. But what terrible thing
has happened *lately?*

At the end of Jessica Mitford's book on the trial of the "Boston

Five," she has Dr. Spock standing, his arms beseechingly outstretched saying, "Wake up, America." I remember thinking as I read it, "If America does wake up, you're dead, dad; head for the hills." Blackstone and John Lewis, of course, would ask, "But which America you'all talking about?"

6   Resistance Fights Back

The work of rediscovery is not quite finished. We have penetrated the disfiguration, stripped away the disguise furnished by the criminality charge, and have refound the primary issue. It has fresh historical moment on being rediscovered. Yes indeed, there are two Americas and one is at the mercy of the other. And the sub-America is ringed with policemen whose guardlike presence leads the subpoor, sub-black, sub-Americans to consider their life a jail, to be endured, birth a sentence to which appeal is impossible and reprieve all but unthinkable. When criminality is added on to the load of subcitizenship and subpoverty these poorest of all have suffered more than a new burden. Criminality dismisses consideration of the problems they constitute by ordering a thunderingly righteous campaign against them, thereby further obscuring their plight. But the constitutional question has not died. It emerges with new vigor. Can the republic continue to confer citizenship on some and deny it to others—and still be called a republic?

The attempt to transform these (technical) citizens into a criminal problem was a brilliant success with the news media and public opinion at large. It has yet to be considered within the sub-American sector. At once, the people there look upon the efforts as ready confirmation of what they have known all along and as not different from past experience except in respect to the new intensity they see in the effort. The effort has become a campaign. Any notion of an utterly passive population beyond the blue curtain was dispelled forever by the tumultuous violence which erupted in almost all metropolitan areas of the country in the latter half of the 1960s. So these people are not abstract eyes perceiving a campaign materializing against them. Having nothing, they have literally nothing to lose. They fight, in a word. When the law is manipulated to make them appear criminal, then they say hell-no to the law. When policemen begin concentrating their force, resistance concentrates itself and tenses for a battle. It is not a matter of resistance losing respect for the law and its officers, since there never was any respect. The people in sub-America already know about policemen. The people cannot be said, accurately, to have given up on the system, either, for the plain reason they never had any system to give up. City Hall is as remote as Washington. The agents of City Hall, whether agency workers, politicians, or detectives, are considered as one: spies, enemies, and, if black, traitors.

The campaign does make things worse in this part of the world because new fears and new dangers are added to the old ones. And resistance must struggle in new ways, as well, which is the point I shall be wanting to deal with in a moment. The only right the people have is challenged by the campaign, so becomes more important. This is the right they confer on themselves, each to himself, one by one, and it is the right to survive. Survival until tomorrow morning is the goal. Since the campaign presents new threats to that right, it is conferred the more earnestly. It becomes new energy for resistance. "Let the mothers come on. Do their meanest shit. Blackstone win every time." To win means to continue surviving.

Practically the single most enduring sign of subpoverty is hunger. The guys were always hungry. They invited themselves to any eating going on at the church and raided the kitchen almost as a right. For all the stories of the big money Rangers were making in their various criminal activities, they were always out of a quarter to buy a hamburger which would be all they ate that day. They were always looking for a way to get money. I could be tempted to rename them "Blacksomebread Rangers" because that was their constant lament: "Some bread, man, gotta find me some bread." The thrilling reading material in the campaign against them would lead a reader to suppose they would buy hamburgers with one of the numerous fifty-dollar bills in their pockets. That is what makes the campaign a new burden. The Stones never did have much chance to get money. The campaign removed even that slim chance.

On many occasions I know of, the Stones sought employment and were refused. An individual Stone, by his own initiative, could get work. He had to lie. He had to disguise his membership in the organization. Stones as Stones had been in so many promising deals which fell through that it was simply apparent, without further consideration, they were not going to get work as Stones.

A potentate of a big steel company, for instance, had sworn he would hire Blackstone Rangers. He gave his word. He asserted positively, as though making a pledge, he was going to hire Blackstone Rangers, knowing that they had criminal records and were most likely dropouts. He was excited, it seemed, about destroying the myth of industrial racism. The deal was set. A dozen Rangers showed up at this company's employment office the next day at the appointed time. They had been briefed on how to fill out the information questionnaire. That was a waste of time. Three of the Rangers were called into separate booths to be interviewed. They were asked their names; then they were asked their addresses. "6502 Blackstone," they said, or an address equally rotten. The interviews ended; no more questions; no jobs; don't come back. The other Rangers walked out with the first three. Their addresses were no better.

Something obviously happened between the green light on the phone one day and the red light in the employment office the next day. A Woodlawn address indicated they were Rangers, but they had come out to the employment office under the direct impression that they were going to be hired because an officer of the company expressly wanted to hire Rangers. The Rangers knew instantly what had happened. "Somebody blowed the deal for us. Goddamn Gang Intelligence, probaly."

Many similar reversals happened. Most of the time, however, employers did not give the first go-ahead; they more honestly refused to discuss the absurdity of hiring Rangers, since the papers were full of the campaign against them. Because it enjoyed such prominence in the campaign and represents more clearly than any other single event the effects of the campaign on the Rangers and their response to those effects, the story of the T.W.O. Job Training Project deserves telling. T.W.O. and the federal government made a mass effort to spring both Rangers and Disciples into steady work.

The president of The Woodlawn Organization (T.W.O.) in 1967–68 was the Reverend Arthur M. Brazier, pastor of the Apostolic Church of God in Woodlawn. He became interested in getting funded a program for neighborhood youth when the Office of Economic Opportunity in Washington, represented by Jerome Bernstein, turned down T.W.O.'s proposal to O.E.O. for the total renovation of Woodlawn. Bernstein expressed interest in the component of that proposal labeled "Neighborhood Youth." Bernstein said, "But cut the crap out of the proposal. You are talking about Rangers and Disciples. Call them by their real names. They may be a lot of things but they sure are not neighborhood youth." What might be done for, with, or by Rangers and D's? Bernstein advised: "Recreation is a loser; neighborhood improvement is a loser; community beautification is a loser; housing is too expensive; jobs is your winner." —Open letter to Tom Wolfe: You wrote in your book about the Rangers' job training program. In fact these are the very words you wrote:

Some of the main heroes in the ghetto, on a par with the Panthers even, were the Blackstone Rangers in Chicago. The Rangers were so bad, the Rangers so terrified the whole youth welfare poverty establishment, that in one year, 1968, they got a $937,000 grant from the Office of Economic Opportunity in Washington. The Ranger leaders became job counselors in the manpower training project, even though most of them never had a job before and weren't about to be looking for one. This wasn't a case of the Blackstone Rangers putting some huge prank over on the poverty bureaucrats, however. It was in keeping with the poverty program's principle of trying to work through the "real leaders" of the black community. And if they had to give it to the protective coloration of "manpower training," then that was the way it would have to be done. Certainly there was no one who could doubt that the Blackstone Rangers were the most powerful group in the Woodlawn area of Chicago. They had the whole place terrified. The Rangers were too much. They were champions. . . . The police would argue that in giving all that money to gangs like the Blackstone Rangers the poverty bureaucrats were financing criminal elements and helping destroy the community. The poverty bureaucrats would argue that they were doing just the opposite. They were bringing the gangs into the system.*

These words describe an idealism driving poverty bureaucrats which may actually exist. These words do not describe an idealism in one of those bureaucrats, named Jerome Bernstein, the very one who funded the Rangers project. He combined cynicism with wit in a way which I am sure would have amused you, Tom Wolfe. Job training for Jerome Bernstein was, in his words, "a masterful way to throw a fuck right in Daley's ear, so he will be sure to hear it." Tilt your passage about forty-one degrees to the port and it will be, as ever, just right.—

Following Bernstein's suggestion, T.W.O. perfected a proposal to introduce Rangers and D's to the world of steady work. At that point Arthur Brazier asked to have a meeting with Ranger leaders arranged in order to describe the proposal to them. When he met with the Mains he quickly learned two important facts. They rejected the proposal immediately because they had had nothing to do with preparing it. And they treated as fact their knowledge that, if they were to have a part in constructing a "really boss" proposal, it wouldn't amount to a thing. "No one's gonna let Rangers in to work." They insisted it had nothing to do with alienation or showing up late (the psychological and practical theories most often used to explain why they were not getting and /or keeping jobs). The Mains insisted jobs were one way out of prison and the guards wouldn't allow prisoners to leave. Even a resourceful and convincing Arthur Brazier could not budge them away from their "parochial" view. He reported this to Bernstein, who agreed completely with the Mains.

*Radical Chic and Mau-Mauing the Flak Catchers (New York: Farrar, Straus, and Giroux, 1970), pp. 140–1.

The proposal made a big turn after that meeting. T.W.O. allowed Ranger and Disciple leaders to make an "input" into the thinking. They said, "Supposin' there is jobs [to indicate their opinion it was impossible to be thinking this way] then the trick's to git the fella to go to his gig and when he git there to keep any fuckers there from messin' with him." A plan was developed which accounted for these types of problems, which, in turn, was translated into proposalese. Here was the plan.

Job trainees would be paid forty-five dollars a week. They would proceed through three stages. In stage one a trainee would go to a center and upgrade his mathematics and literacy skills to an eighth-grade level. No matter where his skills were when he entered, he would have an individual tailored program to get him to the required level in the shortest possible time. Machine learning devices would be used.

In stage two a trainee would move into an on-site training program devised by an employer. The employer would be subsidized. The employer would determine when the trainee was sufficiently trained to do the job he was learning.

In stage three a trainee would move onto the actual job and would thereafter be paid the going rate for that job. His weekly stipend would then be terminated.

The plan called for supervisors who would be related to the trainees through all three stages. But the supervisors were not going to be professional educators or social workers. The supervisors were going to be Rangers and D's. The power of that relationship would then be used to make the whole program work in all stages. A Main says to a Ranger, "You show up at seven in the morning," the trainee will probably show up at six forty-five to make sure. No lolly-gagging around in bed after the alarm goes off, not with a Main on one's tail. A Main says, "Learn that shit, Jack," and Jack turns toward his machine-teacher with gusto. No questions. No backtalk. No resistance. A trainee gets hassled in stage two or stage three and the Main is on hand to straighten the thing out.

It was a "boss" proposal, all right. It got funded, too, but not without difficulty. It ran into heavy trouble from the start. It was opposed by the entire youth-serving establishment in the City of Chicago. Gang Intelligence Unit spokesmen deplored the very idea and predicted that such a project would contribute to increased criminality. The Chicago O.E.O., Y.M.C.A., Boys' Clubs, Commission on Youth Welfare, Streets Program, joined by G.I.U., mounted an active campaign against it. They used their heavy Democratic leverage on national O.E.O. director, Sargent Shriver—an old Illinois politican. They presented "evidence" of a sorts to senior O.E.O. officials in the hopes they would be warned away from dealings with criminal gangs. In a final desperate effort, they contrived a brand-new all-city program called "Youth Action," designed to provide recreational and job-placement opportunities to ghetto youth. But that program did not achieve its desired result. Neither Rangers nor D's would be disposed to anything short of resisting that kind of program. All efforts proved ineffective against an idea whose time had come. It got funded, that "boss" proposal. The day following its annuncement, Bernstein came to Chicago for initial meetings with T.W.O., Ranger, and Disciple leaders. No sooner had the meeting begun than Edward Buckney himself broke in with the announced intention of arresting everyone in the meeting. He did not succeed, since Bernstein was in the back room and had some leverage of his own to use against Buckney. He had been unsuccessful in stopping its funding, therefore he set about wrecking it—an intention portended in the June 6, 1967, raid on the first meeting of Project people.

In September Gene Hairston was arrested and charged with murder. In October Jeff Fort was arrested and charged with murder. In November five Mains were arrested and charged with rape. Each of these police actions was related in the abundant press coverage to the job-training project. The *Chicago Tribune* particularly was incensed over the idea of federal funds being spent on a project whose personnel were being charged with murder and rape.

Before stage one was well begun, there was no longer any stage three, and , of course, stage two. Those employers once ready to destroy the vestiges of corporate racism suddenly contracted *out*. The announcement of the murder and rape arrests had not gone unnoticed. They reported to T.W.O. officials that they couldn't go through with the project because their employees wouldn't stand for it, they were frightened of working with criminals, and so on. So, with the flick of an arrest, the Project was literally killed.

Ironically, no list bearing the names of these employers can be found. They have dropped into anonymous bad faith. I think, in my more somber moods, there never was a list. There never were employers with imagination enough to have signed up in the first place. This would require me to believe that T.W.O. officials pretended to the fellas that the employers had backed out, when, in fact, they had never backed in. I don't believe that, however. I *know* the list of employers cannot be found.

Efforts were made to restore the Project. The Urban League of Chicago was given a subcontract to produce job slots and could come up with no better than what a guy could find in the want ads on his own. The whole plan depended on there being a stage three when a trainee signed up. This was what the Ranger leaders insisted on. With a stage three, a trainee, the first thing, is taken to the plant where he is eventually going to work. He is shown all of those happy people working in the plant making their $4.59 an hour, doing that cool stuff with the little machines and tools and stuff, going to the cafeteria for that dynamite food, laughing and joking with each other. The supervisor with the trainee says, "Well, trainee, how does that grab ya?" Inspired, you see, the trainee rushes back to his machine-teacher and works like a madman to get out there and stash away some of that great bread. When the trainee has no plant to visit, no $4.59 an hour to aim toward, well, "Forget you, stupid." Who is going to be fool enough to diddle away on the little teaching machines? Project officials discouraged gloomy thinking (more "victim image reification") and kept pointing to the likelihood of a stage three and stage two rematerializing. But the Stones knew the prison too well. As soon as the "Bull" was picked up, the Stones knew totally, without reservation, "It's over, Jack."

The Project wound itself down, pretending to be going on. The McClellan Committee was incensed over reports of hanky-panky with the timesheets. The fellas were said to have signed each other's names to the timesheets without showing up in the stage one centers, there to endure the inanities of stage one headed for no further stages. The fellas were reported to have signed each other's names to their weekly paychecks—not an uncommon occurrence among people without identification (or verifiable names presently being used), hence without means to get checks cashed. But with the G.I.U. interpreters close by to point out what it meant, this signing each other's names to checks turned out to mean a vast kick-back scheme designed to enrich gang treasuries. Furthermore, it meant that the fellas were gouging the federal government with clear and criminal fraud. A federal grand jury was eventually convened and pored over these irregularities—the fraud, the hanky-panky, the not going to school, the not getting jobs, the check misendorsing—and after five months came up with 132 indictments against twenty-four Stones, and, lucky for the grand jury, came up with another George Rose-type "stool pigeon"—star witness. The trial was conducted in 1972. The record of the trial might well have been written by Franz Kafka, one assumes, supported probably by Terry Southern, it was that preposterous. Three Stones finally were found guilty of *conspiring* to defraud the government.

One wonders when a tribunal will be appointed to investigate the cost of bringing these three poorest of all to "justice," a cost in certain excess of one million dollars. One wonders as well when a tribunal will be appointed to try the bad faith of the employers who destroyed the Project. After all, the government sank another one million dollars into a project which these employers literally destroyed, wasting, thereby, a good deal of taxpayers' money. The tribunal might profitably explore the intimate relationships between the employers' actions and the direct efforts of Chicago Police Department officials to make clear the meaning of the sensationally criminal charges lodged against the Stone leaders. What might be further examined is the fact that none of the charges was sustained. Gene Hairston was found guilty of the minor conspiracy charge, but not guilty of the murder charge. Jeff Fort's case was dropped before it came to trial for want of sufficient evidence to prosecute. The five Stones accused of rape, similarly, never had to go to trial.

It is beside the point to speculate whether or not the Project might have worked. Who will know whether or not the Stones might have meshed into some straight working deal? They had one apparently clear chance at the prospect. It got busted. No other plans will be tried, one feels safe in predicting.

The short-term advantage sought by the police in keeping Stones out of employment is understandable. The police were seeking to blunt the power of the gangs. The police expected that the gangs would use the actual salary money they made in the Project to strengthen the gang structure; moreover, the gang reputation for ability to deliver advantages to gang members would be enhanced were high-paying jobs another advantage to be offered.

The short-term advantage produces long-term consequences. The young men in the gangs (whose power has thus been blunted, according to police thinking) might very well look upon the police power-show and reconsider the whole matter of their continued membership in the gangs. This was the effect desired by the police. A display of police determination would wake them up, shake them up perhaps, and make them think twice about further gang activities. But, and it seems odd to have to note it, most of the young men do not think in the same way policemen do. The fellas looked upon the police power-show as a confirmation of their view of the world. Police action did not stir up reflection; it aroused rage. And in the meantime, the old wolf is at the door. The "some bread" endures as a daily question. What are they going to do? That is the sober question to be raised. Even straight ghetto youth can't always find work. The unemployment rates for unskilled black youth are notoriously the highest in the country. A Stone is not even up to belonging in those rates, since he is super-unemployed.

The long-term consequence produced by the police campaign is to force the Stone into what he can find, short of starving to death, of course. And there is something to find: a flourishing job market maintained by criminal industries located right on his block. Put in its rational form, the proposition is absurd: fight crime by forcing crime to happen. A crime-fighting policy which drives people to criminal work seems at best ill-thought and perhaps demonic. But that is necessarily what had to happen. There is work to do, never fear. There is dope to be pushed; there is alchoholic beverage to be sold below cost since it bears no revenue stamp; there is the business of getting prostitute and prostituted into the same bed; there is hot merchandise to be bought, sold, handled, delivered; there is protection needed for wire rooms and numbers wheels; there are contracts ready to burn down buildings, shoot people, strong-arm, protect, deliver; there are hustles to be engaged in, robberies to be executed, a thousand deals for the right boy. These criminal industries do not ask questions. They pay well and in cash. Furthermore, they seem to be favored by the police with protection.

That is how the "some bread" question might be answered. A Stone has to live. He is not always at a meeting or out on the street in a confrontation. He requires food and clothing. Likely he has a lady and children who have the same needs. Yes, the police have definitely tried to force him out of the Stones so that he will join the multitudes of noncriminal Americans scrabbling for an honest dollar—except, the police action forbids his scrabbling and forbids the honest dollar. Whether or not a Stone *would* join that multitude has been cast aside. He can't.

If the police intended to break up the Stones in breaking up the Job-Training Project, they failed. Resistance continued, augmented with fresh rage. The Stones had set out on the Project with practical "some bread" goals. It was temporary money. It would maybe wake T.W.O. up and make this community organization aware of the difference between regular underprivilege and under-underprivilege. It might provide occasions which would gather support for the Nation. These goals were interrupted by a flurry of hopefulness that they might really make it into the land of comfort and plenty ($4.59 an hour). After those hopes were blasted, the Stones returned to the old goals fashioned in resistance. They wouldn't get jobs but they would surely make it clear what a filthy "game" G.I.U. had "switched" on them, which practically amounts to an end in itself.

All told the Stones sought to enter the restaurant business on three occasions. They did not succeed in any of them. What they wanted and what they got from the police by way of an answer are the same kinds of things which are by now almost predictable.

There was a lunch-counter restaurant on 63rd Street. The Stones found it was in an area which would be torn down in a few months or years to make way for urban renewal. The operator of the restaurant wanted to get out while he could. The Stones decided they wanted to get in. Since you have not seen the First Church kitchen after extensive Stone use, you therefore will not be able to understand how dumfounded Chuck Lapaglia was when he first heard about the restaurant proposal. He was frank: "Well, if you do get it, you can count on one customer you are never going to see." (The kitchen was a sticky subject.)

Conversation produced the information that the Stones were not interested in the eating part of the restaurant business. They were fascinated by the *location* of the restaurant. As they explained it to Chuck, this place was only a few steps away from the last station on the Jackson Park Elevated. "All those peoples walkin' by." It was only those same few steps away from a major bus transfer point. "All those peoples walkin' by." But more important, it was only a half block away from Hyde Park High School. All Woodlawn students would go right by the restaurant in order to get to and away from school. *And,* it was in the neighborhood of one of the more fabulous whorehouses on the south side. It was a perfect location.

Chuck could see the politics of the location, well enough. But, as I recall, he could not see the business of running the restaurant being taken care of. "Let's be sensible," he said. "People have to be out of bed at seven o'clock in the morning. They have to cook. They have to have food to cook. They have to order the food to cook. They have to do a lot of stuff which is called running a business. You guys can't run water out of the sink."

Jeff Fort, not upset at all, said, "No problem. No problem atall. I gotta Stone lined up who know the business. He been workin' in the Loop a long time doin' that, how-do-you call-it?, runnin' water outa the sink. He be the manager. Ready to go."

So be it. What is wrong with the idea? What is wrong with these Stone black Horatio Algers making a run at Howard Johnson? Why shouldn't they get into business? Stone ideas began to go off like skyrockets. They eventually could envision a black "Old Town" where the cool rich people would come and buy the cool black stuff ready to be sold. One could almost hear a fife and marimba duet beginning in the background, whacking out a funky "Stars and Stripes Forever."

The necessary arrangements were made and a short-term lease gave Stones the restaurant. They began painting it and planning for a gala grand opening. On the second painting day the phone in the church office rang. It was one of the painters.

"The man said you'all can't have a restaurant goin' on in here."

Ann answered, "What man said that?"

"The inspector fella."

"But there already is a restaurant there."

"He said you'all can't have a restaurant goin' on in here. Do we keep paintin'?"

The church staff tried to determine what the difficulty was. An inspector had been in the restaurant and had found it unlicensable. A reinspection was requested and granted.

A team of Stones and Ann were in the restaurant when the inspector appeared. He began looking around and making check marks on a form. He was asked what he was doing, and he said he was noting the condition of the building. He also said that the building should be torn down and did not come near meeting code requirements. That was certainly true enough. Everything about the place was in violation of code. The plaster was falling down. The electric wiring was exposed at points and rotten. The plumbing was inoperative. The counter was worn. The steam tables were dangerous. The dishwasher missed temperature minimum standards by thirty degrees. The stoves had never been cleaned, apparently. The refrigerator was damaged and would be a germ-catcher. "What else do you want to know, Miss?" The Stones and Ann insisted that those problems were fixable. They would all be fixed in three weeks. "Why not come back in three weeks and look at the place again?"

The inspector, very tired, almost kindly, said, "Take my word for it, Miss. If you refinish the place in glazed tile and stainless steel and put in brand-new equipment and sterilize the whole thing with Lysol spray every thirty seconds, it wouldn't make any difference. You—aint—gonna—get—a—license."

Ann thanked him for explaining all of that to them and tried to move the negotiation onto a more positive and informal basis.

"Look," she said, "a restaurant was going on here a week ago, just like you see it now except now there's some new paint on the walls. Everything you see is just like it was then. It didn't run down in a week." She got up from a stool and walked over to the wall. There was a current Board of Health license in a frame. She took it down from the wall and showed it to the inspector. "There is a valid license for this year issued by your department."

The inspector didn't look at the license. He was angry. He had tried to be kind. He said, "I don't have to take your shit." And he walked out.

A detective from the G.I.U. saw some of the guys on 67th Street that night and asked, "When's the restaurant going to open?" and laughed the laugh of the victorious.

It was clear. G.I.U. blocked the restaurant. It is now clear the Stones wanted to have a restaurant, in part, so that G.I.U. detectives would grind their teeth in rage every time they drove by. Beyond that, a restaurant would be an ideal focal point to do business with the peoples going by on the sidewalk. And, it must not be ignored, they might also make "some bread," or cook some.

The situation was not really ambiguous. It seems that way. It seems a fierce resistance outfit would not consent to dirty its ideological hands with these capitalist schemes. But this fierce resistance outfit was ready to make a run at success anytime. It would not make it, it knew. A wall would appear. Then the outfit could say, "Look at that wall. We been right all along. No way we git outa here." This was the unfailing component of their resistance: to show, to educate, to alert. It almost amounted to a countercampaign, conducted, however, deep in the ghetto, among the already enraged, stirring the peoples up against the Man and otherwise "givin' 'im fits." Little wonder the City of Chicago hated them so passionately.

Part Three

The Re-emergence of the

Lower-than-Poor as Outlaws

Among the defiant lower-than-poor, the campaign against them is viewed as ready confirmation of what they have known all along. Regular American is against them. They resist the campaign with spectacular public displays. How can they be criminals when they are not even citizens? They will not be contained. They storm out into public view, their disregard for conventions of social conflict confirming underlying fears that they will ruin the country. Once seen in their fury it is clear they are dangerous outlaws who must be thrown into prison, and never mind about due process. The great question does not perish for having been imprisoned, however. It gains strength for an outbreak—someday.

7   "Stone 'em; the Onlyest Way"

outlaw, n.1. One who by legal process has been put out of the protection and deprived of the benefit of the law in every respect; a person who by reason of crime has forfeited all civil rights and is civilly dead. 2. A lawless, disorderly person; a habitual lawbreaker, especially one who openly defies the law, as a bandit. 3. *Eng. law* A person outlawed by process. 4. (Western U.S.) Vicious; untamable, said of horses.*

The metamorphosis of sub-America into criminal America, seen in the metamorphosis of Blackstone from a powerful youth organization into a criminal gang, has proved unstable. It was unsatisfactory no less than inaccurate. The people who *are* the sub-America, Blackstones's peoples and Blackstone itself, positively go out of their way to resist it and to make a shambles of its pretentious simplism. "We are *not* criminals," they say with not a little asperity and violence. "You got us wrong," they seem to say. "We are people first of all, still outside looking in and you are going to have to deal with us some way someday."

The issue endures; it was first unutterable poverty; in its new appearance it is reuttered poverty. At one time it was quiet resistance going on between people and policemen. In its new form it is wide-

Funk and Wagnalls New Standard Dictionary. Used with the permission of Funk & Wagnalls Publishing Co.

open, spectacularly public resistance, at once frightening and demanding. No one can come away from a really *bad* Stone public appearance with the idea these guys are a gang. They are, as one nonplussed citizen put it, "an army." There will be no more staying inside the compound. The issue has re-emerged on the streets, unrelenting, boiling mad, and portending a violence far beyond mere criminality, which was only their shooting each other. Perhaps this was buried in the criminality issue as its driving force. Chicagoans, with the ready-made perceptions afforded them by police and press, looked out upon all of that unchecked raping, robbing, thugging, kniving, mauling, shooting, murdering, dope-crazed bunch of maniacs and feared it would reach out and . . . gottcha! Chicago is no longer safe for decent people; Negroes are ruining the city; and IT'S A SHAME.

That was probably it all along. The city wasn't interested in crime, it was interested in saving its own neck from violence. Thus, when the issue started blasting through the blue curtain in unmistakable ways, right out into public view, with no detectives needed to point out what perfectly good eyes could see, there was no reason to doubt anymore who these people are. They are just plain outlaws. And Blackstone, Blackstone's peoples, their counterparts in every America city would have to agree with that definition, enthusiastically. That is exactly what they are. So the issue finally came into focus for what it had been all along, although one can see dimly that quite different understandings of that word "outlaw" are operating in the looking-at and the looked-at.

i

On the Sunday afternoon after Martin Luther King, Jr., had been murdered, the Stones and Disciples cooperated in a gala march for peace through the Woodlawn community, which had *not* rioted due to their express efforts to control even riots. Three thousand Stones and 300 Disciples marched in honor of the peace Dr. King had championed. They marched under the guns of National Guardsmen, past an infuriated G.I.U. which had sought in vain to prohibit the march (as dangerous), and in front of the citizens of Woodlawn who openly admired "their boys" for the first time. The guys marched through 63rd Street and then headed for the "midway"—a grassy, block-wide open space between the communities of Hyde Park and Woodlawn. On the Woodlawn side of the midway, observing the peace being talked and done by the fellas, were a happy lot of people, glad the place was still whole and openly proud that the fellas had had the nerve to slick the authorities right out in the light of day.

On the other side of the midway were the people of Hyde Park, whose community had not even been eligible for riots, of course, and so who were not particularly jubilant about what they were seeing on the midway. Hyde Parkers looked across all of those Stones, who were steadfastly looking across the Hyde Parkers looking, and they saw social catastrophe. To them, it looked like James Baldwin's fire had come this time. It was a frightening experience. One matron said, "So this is the Blackstone Rangers. I thought they were, well, younger somehow and more evil looking, you know, like a real menace should look." Her companion mused further, "It is hard to believe they are as bad as people say. I don't know how this sounds, but, you know, they are very good-looking boys." They hadn't seen the real article before, having been served up caricatures in the news media and in cocktail-party gossip. When Hyde Parkers saw real Stones in front of them, 3,000 strong, they would never again believe in a relatively simple description of the Stones as mere criminals. A good many of them, perhaps a majority of those on the north side of the midway that Sunday, developed some new fears beyond the worst possible fears. "If they can stop a riot from starting, they can start one anytime they want to. They are sure as hell no gang. They are an army." One may well believe that ward committeeman Marshall Korshack got his ear full that night.

The characteristic of these outbreaks is the purest resistance, for it is wide-open, unambiguous, *declared* defiance. As outbreak, these events burst the boundaries of conventional thinking and forced new, truer, harder definititons as a replacement for the too-simple criminality charge. But, one sees, the matter is by no means crystal clear. The outbreaks were not constructive activity. They were not a species of "doing good." They were a species of doing *control*, and thereby of displaying strength. Furthermore, they were not public spectacles, to be viewed as dramatic productions. They were calculated emergences of a real strength gathered among the peoples all of the time, and already there. The Stones deliberately intended onlookers to draw the conclusion they could do this any time they chose, next Tuesday morning, or whenever another occasion might demand it. For this organization, if an army, is not called up, like the National Guard, for an emergency. It is always called up in its strength and ready for anything.

The Stone explanation is, "Stone run it," which is a resistance idea, as we earlier pondered its meaning. But it is also a control idea. "Stone *control* it"; "Stone control what's goin' on round here"; "Stone gotta eye on all that be happenin'"; "Stone be seein' the whole scene"; "Stone know"; "Stone *is* the peoples; Stone not always sayin' stuff for peoples to do like they be scared not to do it, Stone always sayin' what the peoples wants and needs"; finally, "Stone run it don't mean no-thin' but Stone love."

Therefore, when Stones erupt from obscurity into public view, the obscurity is not different from the public appearance. That is what the Stones want onlookers to *know*. On the block and on the midway is one and the same thing. It is an especially important point to make for those onlookers who have never been on the block and therefore have no way to estimate their enduring strength.

One might with profit find a map of the city of Chicago and study it. The Stone area begins along the line represented by the Stevenson Expressway (I-55) and stretches southward all the way beyond the Chicago city limits, past Harvey-Dixmoor, on to Chicago heights or about 250th Street. The western boundary of the area is generally State Street, although the area juts west of State Street between 43rd Street and 63rd Street. This is the CobraStone territory. The eastern boundary is Lake Michigan until it sweeps eastward at Jeffrey Avenue. Jeffrey Avenue then represents the boundary as it runs south.

One can see this is a vast area. It is the area the Stones claim they run. They say every poor black kid in this entire area, boy and girl, big enough to be on the street is in the Stone system, passively or actively, because the Stone system is in the street before they get there. It is in the street, playgrounds, public parks, shopping areas, schools, and alleys. Lots of not-so-poor black kids are actively in the system. And some other not-so-poor black kids not in the system have split heads or live with an auntie in Detroit. To be black and poor and kid means being Stone. Mama doesn't like it a bit and the kid will tell Mama, "They made me. Said they'd kill me if I didn't join," but that's for Mama, to soothe her nerves. The kid has been Stone all his life. He couldn't be kept out.

A heavy Stone walks into a store-coke shop-ribs shack-hang place in a marginal area. He has come to remove the marginal. It is five o'clock in the afternoon. The place is full of kids. He raps his walking stick on the floor. "Stone love," he says, louder than the juke box is saying, "Onnnne less bell to answer." Someone has pulled its plug. Once more, louder, he says, "Stone love." He then looks around the room slowly, as if to fix each feature of each face of each kid in his mind. Minutes have gone by. The room is quiet. He now says, "Stone comin' in here. This be Stone City from now on." After a long suggestive pause he adds, "I be goin' outside." The kids can't wait to get out of that store fast enough to join him outside. The store keeper better be hip, too; he better not say, "Hey, wait a minute, you didn't pay." He is in Stone City now.

The heavy Stone starts taking inventory outside. He is not alone. There are other Stones with him, finding out who these peoples are, where they go to school, who the polices are, where the action is. In time a meeting is announced and the heavy Stone leaves along with all but one of his companions. He stays there. He is the resident Stone; he is an "Ambassador." The Stones have landed.

For the Stones this activity is good all by itself, without reference to anything else. This is the classic *Ranger* stuff. This is making the organization available. It is evangelism. It is offering salvation to lost souls. It is throwing a rope to people going down in quicksand. What chance do these kids have, whiling away their time in that corner store, if the Stones don't come in? "They gonna go to school all their lives, git their minds messed up with a lota white shit? They gonna be out there shootin' up dope? They gonna be on their knees before the polices, suckin' off their cocks? They gonna be hopin' for a job they git cut way from in two weeks? What chance they got, less'n we come in here and put some Stone in their black heads, make 'em mens?"

It is not the intention of the heavy Stone and the assigned Ambassador to force everyone in that area to become members of the Black P. Stone Nation. There will be new members enough without having to push anyone around. It is the intention of the heavy Stone to stake the marginal area out and claim it. In that act he lets all the kids know who is boss in this area. There will be Stone business going on and all of those kids better be hip, as the storekeeper better be hip. A Stone needs help, they better be ready to help; and if they need help, they know who to look for. It works both ways. The Stones demand respect for their business and are ruthless about getting it. But, every sub-poor, abused, messed-over human being in that area has got a champion, as well. If the storeowner gets in trouble, he is going to know Stones will help him. If he messes with the kids, or gets "slick" with the police, then he had better move, right now.

One way or another, every poor black kid in the whole area is in the Stone system. The kids are part of it actively as members of the Nation, or passively because they have no choice (but to move to Detroit). Generally the control is loose. Normal life goes on. Sometimes the control becomes very tight. An issue arises in the school, perhaps, or the police come looking for someone, or a pusher has violated an agreement. Whatever the occasion, the tight control means the area suddenly locks tight. The school, for instance, becomes a strict Stone school, and the student body acts the way a Main tells it to act. The authority of administration, parents, and police are nothing compared to the authority of the Main. Ordinarily, the school just has a lot of Stones going there. But at times it is also a Stone school. And if the matter is the police looking for someone the Stones don't want found, the police run into solid resistance. Let them break heads, rant and rave, fire off a whole clip from their automatic; not even eleven-year-old kids are impressed. They remain quiet with that insulting, infuriating calm of theirs. And if a pusher has decided to put the firepower of his organization against the Stones, "Better go inside awhile, Dad."

But tight control is only occasionally necessary. Most of the time the control is loose and easy. Normal life goes on. And that is a life that by suburban standards is violent, by leagal standards is criminal, and by white standards is frankly immoral. Whether Stones or not, kids without money or legitimate ways to get money, pick up the available in order not to starve. So do their mothers. So does everybody. There it all goes on, like it has for decades—since the city lured cheap labor from the south. No one particularly cares about it or seems interested in changing it. Even after the publication of the Kerner Commission Report, and after the publication of roughly 4,700 classy paperback books detailing the phenomenology of the black fix, especially after the publication of the monumental *Autobiography of Malcom X,* this life continues unchanged. One catches the moralism in official descriptions of Stone criminality when they suggest that the Stones initiated it or perhaps created it. In truth the Stones have come out of it with a determination to display its inutterable inhumnanity to the condemning regular—official—America, which is the other side of their loose and easy control.

Control may be seen to be two definite activities. It is gathering strength among the peoples; it is public display of that strength. They are, of course, intimately related, in fact are so closely bound together that they appear as definite activities only for the purposes of analysis. As it goes on, the activities are one. That is what provided the march for peace on the midway its thirty-two-foot bass with which to shake the very foundations of Hyde Park and the University of Chicago for which it stands. There weren't just 3,000 sullen kids out there. There were 30,000, maybe 300,000, all of them exhibiting their utter defiance and contempt of civilized society. "How does that grabya, Pal?"

Especially should "Pal" consider that they weren't doing one thing illegal or criminal.

ii

A yet more remarkable public display of Stone power occurred in the fall of 1968 after the McClellan hearings fixed on them a reputation for greed and rapacity scarcely paralleled in American history. One misses the peculiar ambience of this event by tying it too closely to national or Chicago history, as calamitous as public events were that fall. This display of power emerged from Stone urgencies, not as a response or a retaliation. It was a "boss" stunt and that is all; its origins deserve note because, though Stones call it more "high-class nonvilence" and "jest doing good for the peoples" it was nevertheless a very big lot of violence to the Cook County Democratic Committee and its illustrious chairman, Richard J. Daley.

The event I refer to is the no-vote campaign conducted in the autumn of 1968. Such a definitely south side organization of sub-Americans could be expected to have no interest in national politics. That surmise is accurate. The Stones had no interest. They had once talked with Robert Kennedy and considered him a "boss cat." Had he been running for the presidency, the Stones might have been mildly interested in the election. Since he was dead, they weren't interested at all. They weren't interested in local politics, if by that is meant the businesss of voting for a local fella. The mayor had that all locked up. They could not work up enough enthusiasm to be angry about his absolute control of local elections. An election provided a momentary bonanza of dollar bills for Stone peoples.

But the Stones began to see the makings of a stunt in 1968. It did not originate in far-reaching analysis of the political campaign shaping up. It was fundamentally a control idea, more of that "high-class nonvilence." The stunt they began to see coming on was "Why vote at all?" Resist the election itself. Later they put a good face on the idea and made it sound like a rational political idea in words of this order: "Nothin' to vote about in this here 'lection. A fool cin see ole

Daley's gonna git hisself more balls 'n ever if his guy wins. Seems like the other guy don't like colored folks atall. Nobody but white dudes runnin'. Let the white folks pick out the guy they want. Us, we be takin' a holiday from votin'." Even as an explicit political option among three, it was not fundamentally a *political* endeavor they were contemplating. It was resistance, pure and simple, They could never beat "ole Daley" at voting; but they could beat him by *not* voting.

After the idea had fully ripened, they got about 600 cans of spray paint and blitzed the Woodlawn and Kenwood areas with a fantastic assortment of political messages. Mostly the messages read, simply, "Don't Vote," or "No Vote." One can see them asking one another, these budding young politicians, "Who sayin' this stuff? Could be Daley hisself sayin' it." The logic was overpowering. The signs thus included a signature. Mostly the signatures were simple statements of fact: "Signed: Black P. Stone Nation," or, if the paint can was getting low, "Signed: B.P.S.N." Some of the more creative signers placed below the message, "Signed: Malcolm X," to indicate, one supposes, that he would have approved of not voting. And, noting T.W.O.'s recent dangerous intimacy with Daley politicians, some of the signers thought of a wicked endorsement, "Signed: T.W.O." Stone faithful tended toward "Signed: The Bull," and "Signed: Angle" ("angle" being the way "angel" is often spelled, referring to the little chief, known to intimates as "Angel").

These signs appeared by the literal hundreds on overpasses, viaducts, underpasses, traffic signs, store windows, the sides of buildings, on the street, across billboards, across both Humphrey and Nixon signs, but mainly on large expanses of brick wall. The south side woke up one morning to a saturation-style message blitz. It created a sensation. It got every black politician and *all* of the older brothers into hurriedly called press conferences to explain that they thought the right to vote had been brought with too much black blood to be thrown away in a tantrum. They said they were going to vote and they urged the black community to vote as well. They didn't explore the matter of whom they were voting for. That was taken for granted.

The Stones followed the paint blitz with outsize Nation meetings in which the election-day action was explained. "You can't be lettin' the peoples in your buildins vote without knowing' they's goin' 'gainst Stone," the spokesmen said. "You wanta rap to your mama and all other peoples and tell 'em they can't vote for Daley or the other guy. Jest stay way from the votin' places and be whistlin' and singin' when the snakes come by try to git 'em down there. A holiday-like, dig? Nothin' heavy." These instructions were put in several different ways but with the same intent. The plan was as simple as the strength it depended on. It was an idea which anybody into resistance would understand instantly. It needn't be explained or argued abut. Stones don't have to carry papers around for peoples to read or get up there on platforms and argue about this and that, issues, racism, the war, law and order—that white stuff. Stones carry ideas which are self-explanatory. Since it was a perfectly rotten idea, anathema to all politicians, all police, all functioning sections of regular America, it must be a good idea for the people so rigorously excluded from regular America.

This was a new one for the machine. It knew how to manipulate totals of votes cast, and to inflate totals. It knew how to manage votes in the act of being cast. It knew how to ensure voters would vote for the ticket. But it didn't quite know how to deal with voters taking a holiday and being quite determined not to vote because of what their children had been saying to them. It didn't know how to deal with people who would take the two dollars and smile and promise and still not vote. The creativity and pocketbooks of precinct captains were strained to produce what vote they did finally muster, which wasn't much. Normally, the Daley machine could expect to get about 90 percent of the registered voters in one of these "low income black" precincts. The machine should have been getting 275 votes in a 300-voter precinct. With urban renewal cutting into a lot of those "low-income black" precincts, the normal 300 figures were more like 180 and 165. The casual observation provided by interested Stones and some of their friends reports that less than 100 voters showed up in the observed precincts. Many of those 100 voters were defiantly announcing to the Democratic captain that they were splitting their tickets in order to show Daley a thing or two. It was a bad day for the machine. It *had* to deliver a 400,000-vote plurality to Humphrey before the downstate Nixon vote started coming in. The machine scarcely produced a 300,000 vote plurality. Humphrey lost Illinois, winning which he would have won the election. Daley had been denied his victory celebration and another four years as a (the?) maker of a president. The Stones could take credit directly for removing 30,000 sure votes from his totals, or, about the size of the Nixon victory in Illinois.

This is "high-class nonvilence." But when they do "good" in such a big way, the Stones scare the city fathers far more than when they are being merely criminal. Official spokesmen publicly ridiculed the effectiveness of the no-vote campaign. To say that a gang had swung the State of Illinois was more than ridiculous, it was blasphemous. But let the spokesmen rattle on in their statements to the press, let the political scientists come up with their analysis of voting profiles, the facts simply will not rub out. The peoples know, the Stones know, and Daley knows (because his precinct captains told him) he got trashed by a gang.

"You gonna deal with us now. We not jivin'; we not gangbangin'; we not off'n D's or nobody. We sicka your shit and you gonna listen." That seemed to be the program. A Stone philosopher mused, however, "Go git peoples stirred up and not votin', you know what the Man be thinkin'? He be thinking' fix up them 'lectric chairs cause lotta Stones be comin' through right away." He was not far from the truth.

What proved frightening to the city in the strength of the Stone organization on the block and in public display was the apocalyptic possibility that the old day was coming to an end. For as many years as there had been a Democratic machine, this machine has depended on the unfailing virtually 100 percent voting performance of the poor black people. If one needs reminding, the "river'" of "river-ward politics" is the Chicago River, running alongside the notorious twenty-fourth (west side) ward. A mixture of lowest American and sub-American residents, these wards represent a gold mine of opportunity. The voters don't care. They are hungry. They can be easily intimidated. They are entirely out of the public debates over "issues" which might or might not be raging in a given election. They don't know or care about issues or candidates. It is a perfect set-up. Once resistance enters, it posits a threat at the very fountainhead of machine power. The Stones perhaps knew these facts dimly. They were surely not set down in a neat analytical row. Somehow, in the stuggle they had found a point of vulnerability and had pressed their advantage.

One can *now* see that when the mayor and the state's attorney stood before the gathered press the following May and announced their war on criminal gangs, they were not just whistling *Dixie*. They had some high-class *violence* of their own to do, some scores to settle . The right of the machine to win elections is the fundamental right in Chicago. It is the capstone of the whole system of rights, hence of civilized society. One had better believe that the hatred welling up in Mayor Daley when he condemned criminal gangs and announced war on them was not a simple function of his concern for the safety of Chicago streets. He was concerned the Stones might do some more of that absolutely legal, clearly public-spirited, and peculiarly violent high-class nonvilence—to *him*.

iii

Eventually the violent truth portended in official minds by these public Stone displays worked itself out for all Chicago to see, although not clearly. Neither the march for peace nor the no-vote campaign was actually violent. They were just frightening. The violence emerged in the summer of 1969.

In the early summer of 1969 Chuck Lapaglia reported, "The Stones have been talking around with some of the brothers. It looks as though they are on to something big. They are getting interested in construction trades stuff. All along they have been talking with Jesse [Jackson], C.T. [Vivian], and Archie [Hargraves]. Lately Buzz Palmer and Renault Robinson [officers of the Afro-American Patrolmen's League] have been in on the talks, too.

"This seems to be the scene: jobs, discrimination, that kind of thing.

Mainly, I guess, they are talking about a common front. It's hard going, too. And I forgot; Kermit Coleman [an attorney with a legal aid service] is in on the talks. It's the old black coalition idea and closer to coming together than it ever has been. There's going to be some heavy flak on this one. It'll be a ball-buster."

Chuck then reported on how the Stones discovered "discrimination" in the building trades. "They went and looked. Edward Bey took along some fellas to count—Edward wouldn't do that little stuff, he supervised the counters. Well, they went around to all of the places where building is going on. They knew it was going on. But it never registered on them how much was going on. You know, there's a hundred million dollars' worth of building going up in Stone territory *today*. They went right into the sites big as you please and added up all the white workers. Then they added up all the black workers. Then they moved on to the next site."

They had wanted to see for themselves. The talks with the brothers had brought the basic facts to light: Historic discrimination, a color bar at entrance into the unions, and a further color bar at the hiring hall, patterns of nepotism and cronyism in union membership and hiring. All of the facts were well known. Except, the Stones did their own head count. It wasn't exactly mistrust for the stated facts and figures. The heavy rhetoric surrounding the facts and figures had aroused ancient Stone suspicions. They mistrusted the old flame-offs who went to Washington Park on pleasant Sunday afternoons and made speeches to each other on subjects like union discrimination. The old duffs wouldn't do anything about it. The Stones mistrusted the reigning black leaders for the same reason. It seemed all too likely they weren't prepared to do anything about the discrimination they liked to excoriate. So the Stones had huffed out of the meeting to do the concrete work.

"The shit start goin' down, those dudes be on an airplane flyin' away somewheres, or be sick, or be at a meetin'." This was the Stone attitude. There are talkers and doers in the world. The talkers won't do; the doers don't talk. The Stones fancied themselves to be among the doers.

One must realize the magnitude of the venture under consideration by the brothers in their "pre-coalition" talk. The same "Irish Tribe" (a term used by Father Tracy O'Sullivan, pastor of St. Clara's Roman Ctholic Church in Woodlawn) which runs city hall, the fire department, the police department, the sanitary district, the parks department, urban renewal, urban progress centers, real estate, shipping, trains, trucking, airplanes, airports, the schools, the newspapers, television, the assessor's office—Chicago—runs big labor and particularly the building trades unions. The journeyman slots in those unions are treated in the same way as city patronage jobs. One must know someone important to get in; someone must "clout" a worker through. To make a big public spectacle of the union color bar was exactly equal to picking a fight with the mayor. He was professionally indebted, after all. The big unions had supported him heavily. Moreover, the union chiefs were among his closest and oldest friends. According to Mike Royko, Daley counts it important that his father was a member of the sheet-metal- workers union.* Daley would have a hand in the fight privately, while corporately, that is, Mayor Daley, as a handy name for an extensive political apparatus—the machine— would fight the open fight.

A fight with the mayor? That is not quite accurate. Hadn't the mayor announced a war against the Stones in May? Hadn't he promised Chicago he would wipe them out? The new venture the Stones were considering was more like a response to a fight the mayor had already announced was underway. This fact of a fight and having to survive it should not be allowed to obscure what the Stones felt to be an important issue in its own right. They knew they weren't going to get any of the jobs that might eventually be won for black workers. Some of the borthers might get some jobs and the Stones knew how low-down poor most of them were. Add the possibility of a functioning coalition with the support and protection it was bound to bring, and the idea seems practically "irresistible."

According to Chuck the conversations of the "precoalition" had

*(New York: E.P. Dutton & Co., Inc., 1972,) *Boss* pp. 67f.

been devoted to tactics. He recollects the older brothers were assured among themselves what the tactics would be. There would be pickets around the construction sites; controlled walks into the sites for confrontation with the foreman or superintendent, or the shop steward; dialogue with union officials and contractors; presentation of demands; negotiations; jobs. He also recollects that the Stones had little to say about these tactics. But as soon as one of those meetings had finished they huddled outside for a moment and decided to have a meeting of their own that night. The meeting began at nine o'clock and finished at two-thirty in the morning. During that meeting the younger brothers worked out the doing part, while the older brothers talked on.

The Stone meeting was not considering the sorts of things which might occur to one while studying the range of feasible tactics; they rejected that picket line, controlled-walk stuff, because, said the commission of on-site counters, supervised so ably by Edward Bey, "Those dudes got hard hats, Jack. Big bellies like polices. BIG mothers, every one. They's mean."

Attention was focused on the very practical matter of how to close down a site full of tough white guys. By their own canons of realism, the Stones ruled out fire and guns. "Seem silly to be burnin' down the building' we tryin' to stop. Can't stop what's not no more." Similarly, "Shoot 'em and some more be back the next day all of 'em with machine guns." The plan they agreed on, though cryptic, is precise: "Stone'em. The onlyest way. Stone 'em right outa there so they wish to God *they* was Stones for a single minute."

To the consternation of the "Precoalition," and its surprise, on the following day 200 Stones, stripped to the waist, or wearing red undershirts recovered from another era, all wearing suns, armed with sticks, boards, pipes, bricks, pieces of concrete, broken bottles, chains, and tire irons suddenly appeared, on the run—and screaming—directly toward the workmen at a Dan Ryan rapid transit construction site. The Stones came over the fence, through the fence, through the gate. The workmen were startled. (One imagines them saying, "What in the hell is happening? Who are these lunatics?") But even though they had no idea what could possibly be going on, if they didn't move instantly, it looked like they might get beaten. They ran to their cars, or some cars, or anywhere out of that site. In a matter of seconds the first site had been shut down for the day, or the duration, maybe, because the Stones yelled to the retreating workmen as they scrambled over the fence that they had better not come back tomorrow, or ever.

This was not a widely reported item on the ten o'clock news that night, which should not be counted strange, despite the anti-Blackstone materials so readily available. Look at it this way. A reporter could say these criminals are resorting to terror in order to impede construction; they are tampering with the private-property rights of builders; they are denying the rights of workers to make an honest living; they are holding up construction on an important rapid transit construction project. And if that were all—if this had been pure hooliganism, rank criminal stuff—then it would have been indeed strange that the news had been omitted from the night news reports. But, much as a reporter might go on and on about the dastardly deed, he couldn't work past the point of the deed forever. Eventually he would have to begin saying why these young gangsters did it. They say black men can't work on that site in the middle of a black neighborhood. "Spokesmen for the Black P. Stone Nation alleged there is widespread discrimination in the building trades unions." That simply destroys the Stones perfectly good and untarnished reputation for pure criminality. So a reporter is wise not to mention that it happened at all.

It was a stunning tactic. The Stones were careful not to repeat the performance exactly. They chose different times of the day to move on other sites. But they always came suddenly, from no place, and if a worker couldn't run fast enough or got mad and started to fight, he got banged. There was talk in the taverns that some workmen were arming themselves for a war. Maybe some of them did begin to carry guns. They didn't, however, use them.

The news which was not getting to the public was getting to union officials and to builders and to City Hall. One surmises they were mutually and equally furious. One also surmises they chose not to protect the remaining sites with solid walls of policemen because the television would zoom right in on the scene of police protecting a bunch of white workers from ghetto toughs who couldn't get a job there, in their own neighborhood. It wouldn't look good. That is surmise. Fact: the police protection so obviously available was not used. So one after another, the sites fell. The Stones had started a caper which the younger brothers all joined as soon as they heard about it. All of the guys—*at that historical moment* being pictured in "Organized Youth Crime in Chicago" as shooting each other dead every fourteenth second—Stones, Disciples, Vice Lords, Young Lords, Latin Lovers, Egyptian Kings, Black Latins, Double Six Kings, Young Patriots, Pharaohs, and, it is said, Black Panthers, got in on the action. It was a beautiful caper. Within a week they had closed down one hundred million dollars' worth of construction, and it wasn't about to be started up again.

The material facts of this blitz began to ooze into public consciousness for the reason that contractors and union officials wanted to resume their business. They had to go to court to get relief from harassment. In a guarded way they admitted to the court that their sites had been invaded and workmen either intimidated or beaten. It was difficult to admit and was never completely admitted, and once out in that fashion, the press began to handle the story.

Attorneys for the builders and unions secured the court order they were after. (The "Irish Tribe" knows how to resume business.) The judge limited pickets to five at a site and prohibited unauthorized entry into all sites.

Where, one might ask, did the pickets come from all of a sudden, who must limit their number to five at a site? Well, they came from the black coalition which had fallen into place. The pickets came from the ladies of Operation Breadbasket and the ladies of the younger brothers, too, preferably ladies with two or three babies with them, and signs full of pathos reading: "MY HUSBAND [FATHER, BROTHER, MAN, SWEETHEART, UNCLE] CAN'T WORK HERE BECAUSE HE IS BLACK." Pickets with signs don't materialize out of thin air. How did they get to the various sites? They were organized. The whole apparatus of the civil rights movement came back to life. "Well, thank God, we can do something again. Here is a cause. We have an issue." Out came the Datsun crowd with bandanas and sunglasses and sensible skirts to march in alongside other sisters whose skirts were absolutely not sensible.

The older brothers had no choice. The success of the Stone tactic had operated like a magnet. The coalition locked into place. Jesse Jackson's Saturday morning meetings of Operation Breadbasket were made into huge evolving rallies for Jobs Now. The younger brothers were treated like heroes. The *Chicago Daily Defender* was right on top of the developing end of racist employment practices. Jobs Now. Decent Jobs for Decent Black Workers. "This is one fight we're gonna win." The older brothers joined reporters in finessing past the "unpleasantness" at the job sites. It was over. Now the real issue can be met. And what is the real issue? "We want the repeal of racist hiring policies. Black people make up 35 percent of the population of this city. We want 35 percent of those union job slots. Not next year or tomorrow, we want them now."

The court order had been handed down in haste to thwart the black coalition's plan to shut down the mammoth construction site at the Circle Campus (of the University of Illinois in Chicago, located on the near-west side). With a coalition managing things, surprise is lost forever. S.C.L.C.-type meetings have to be called to be held in churches. Speakers drum up enthusiasm for new demonstrations. The plan is announced ten different times in ten different ways, in order to enthuse participants. The judge, along with three million Chicagoans out there in TV land, knew about the plan. The judge's order deliberately sought to protect the Circle Campus site.

A showdown loomed.

The coalition's demonstration-picket-rally-shutdown was scheduled to begin at two on a hot afternoon. Well before two the police were at the site in force. It was a block-square site. Contingents of patrolmen with riot gear were stationed at intervals around the site. A large gathering of patrolmen and plainclothesmen, plus newsmen and camera crews were congregated in front of the main gate into the

site whose southern edge was Roosevelt Road—a main east-west
thorough fare. Traffic was being routed away from Roosevelt
Road.

Long before two o'clock there were already more than seventy-five
pickets marching on the sidewalk in front of the site. They were
carrying signs and yelling at police and workmen. They were, of
course, in direct disobedience of the court order but the police made
no move to stop them. Whole busloads of patrolmen in riot gear were
parked down a nearby side street, unobtrusively ready to move in on
any potential developing trouble. The effort to be nonprovocative was
misunderstood. The demonstrators coming up to the front of the site
saw the numbers of police on hand and said among themselves that
the police ought to come right out into the open and fight if that was
that was on their minds. Unmarked police cars full of plainclothesmen
were parked along Roosevelt Road and south on a small side street
which dead-ends on Roosevelt. They had both walkie-talkies and
police radios in the cars crackling with the latest information on the
numbers of demonstrators arriving.

Some of the "younger brothers" began to drift in. The Disciples
were wearing black berets. The Vice Lords and Young Lords wore a
goldish-mustard colored beret. No red berets were to be seen. A group
of Vice Lords had brought their dogs. These dogs were a mangy,
skinny, wild-looking lot, each leashed with a simple piece of flimsy
rope. The dogs were quiet and submitted to petting by children. A
policeman walked nearby and suddenly the dogs went berserk. They
charged, held only by those suddenly insubstantial ropes; they barked,
snarled, and drooled. It required stong fellas to hold them back. They
were laughing, and so was the crowd in the immediate vicinity. The
policemen could not find much to laugh about.

Unattached younger brothers, wearing baseball caps with the bills
turned backward or no hats, came loaded with pieces of concrete,
broken bricks, and stones which were stockpiled directly across the
street from the demonstration. The police made no move to arrest
them, although on other occasions the fellas would not have got
within two blocks of a demonstration with that kind of stuff. It was

clear the police had decided this would be a clean demonstration. They were prepared to arrest anyone trying to get into the site. The people would not be bothered as long as they did not make that attempt.

An hour late, the confrontation got going. Two things happened at the same time. The speakers arrived in a station wagon and the Stones arrived. They marched right down the middle of Rososevelt Road, about 400 of them, led by Jeff, Edward, Sengali, and Chester Evans. No drifting in for them and mixing around with the people. They came on strong and stayed together. The lazy afternoon snapped to attention. Groups of policemen stopped talking and got on their helmets. The Stones wheeled off and stood on the steps and sidewalk in front of a church on the south side of the street. Vice Lord, Disciple, and Young Lord leaders came over for a caucus of the "younger brothers." As they were arriving, Jeff told a Stone named A.D. to take another guy with him and ordered the two of them to stick close to Jesse Jackson. "Make sure he go through the gate and if he don't, throw the sonofabitch over the fence." A.D. got another guy, both of them a lot bigger than Mr. Jackson, who is himself a big man, and they took off.

The speaking started. The Rev. C. T. Vivian got the portable microphone first and let off some salvos about the meaning of the afternoon. He talked about jobs, about stingy unions, about racism, about official racism, about official racism in city hall, about Mayor Daley telling his judge to keep the black folks quiet, telling his police to make the order stick. Since nobody knew what was going to happen, this was pretty hot-sounding stuff. The crowd, police, and press stood listening to find out what was going to happen. Veteran rally-watchers knew that the tip-off was upon them. What does he say next? Does he say, "We're not afraid of the court order, etc."? in which case, pack up your cameras, guys, no show today, or does he say, "Over the fence! This is our ground; those are our jobs!"? He said neither. He embarked on some fiery nonviolence talk. But maybe he wasn't supposed to spill the plan.

On came the big speaker, Jesse Jackson. It is said he can charm snakes out of trees. He said exactly what C. T. Vivian had said, but in such a way that it seemed more thrilling. The evil seemed graver; the protest was more righteous; the cause was surely more just and noble. The demonstration watchers tensed. Here was the point C. T. Vivian had got to. Now Jesse would say it. A hush of sorts developed. Jesse was at the climax. His voice, hoarse with much recent talking, and this very shouting, broke, faltered, thus lending a touching dimension to the closing—lower-key—words, a hoarse, half-whispered yell: "We're gonna win!" Tumultuous applause greeted him.

Having heard Jeff's orders to A.D., one is more than a little interested in the very next seconds. Jesse Jackson had been addressing the crowd from the tailgate of the station wagon. When he had finished, hot, flushed, coughing from the effort (in reality he was in the early stages of pneumonia), he sprang down and started walking toward the front door of the automobile. This was in the right direction, since he was headed toward the gate. But he stopped at the door and was definitely making motions as though he were going to get into the car. The "little chief" hadn't mentioned getting into the car. He had definitely told A.D. to make sure Jesse Jackson went through the gate. So A.D. and his comrade wouldn't let him get into the car. They said, "Through the gate or over the fence," and they were big enough to do it. And in front of the car there were C.T., Chester Evans, Sengali, ready to break the court-ordered injunction. There was the television. There were the police. Hadn't he just finished saying, "We're gonna win!"? It required almost no time to make up his mind to do what had been decided for him to do. He joined the defiance party forming in front of the gate and started to go to jail instead of wherever it was he had been intending to go.

Jeff Fort wanted Jesse Jackson to be in the group which defied the court order. Jeff had not prearranged a plan. He did the plan on the spot. Why? Jesse Jackson is a celebrity. C. T. Vivian is one more black leader. Sengali is a hoodlum Stone. Were these two alone to defy the court order and go to jail, they could stay there indefinitely without another thought being given to them. But Jesse Jackson in jail, to test a hastily drawn, rigged court order, reporters checking up on his condition (he had pneumonia), covering the court hearings (because he is hot copy) means the number-one story in Chicago stays number one. Additionally, the coalititon between older and younger brothers (gangs and respectable black organizations) moves into new strength because of the mutual arrest. Breadbasket people can't lament Jesse's and C.T.'s stay in jail without at least mentioning Sengali's stay. What does that mean? Any eventual talking at some eventual conference table will necessarily include a Stone doing some of the talking. Jeff was simply determined. "The ole fart gonna deal with 'Gali; he not gonna like it; he don't hafta like it. We do the hard stuff gettin' him to hafta talk, by God, he gonna deal with the fellas which do it to 'im." Jeff was referring, of course, to Mayor Daley.

Whatever could they have been thinking of? "Stone 'em; the onlyest way." Perhaps it was "the onlyest way." And no doubt Stones later had many good laughs at the hardhats running in stunned fright to their cars. But it was also the single one thing they could do which would confirm the worst fears about them. They had finally shown the other face of their strength, which is terror. Swollen with rage and fraternal exuberance, they were storming more than a fence at a construction site. They had crossed a historic line. Yes, it was then clear. They are not criminals, for sure. The city had been wrong about that. They were absolute outlaws: "Lawless, disorderly person (s); . . . habitual lawbreaker (s), especially (those) who openly defy the law, as a bandit."

An Operation Breadbasket-sponsored "Black Monday" soon followed the Circle Campus incident. It was held in the Civic Center Plaza beneath the Picasso statue. Memory blurs about who did and who did not speak. It was all interchangable talk anyway. The Stones didn't talk, whether by choice or prohibition one does not know. They were at the rally, a big cluster of suns toward the back of the crowd. City Hall is across the street. There was a solid wall of policemen on the sidewalk, poised between the crowd and the building. Just right and inviting some action, they menaced the eyes glancing over that way. Jeff Fort saw it as an affront to a peaceful assembly. He marched his fellas around, first this way, then that, and finally down the side-walk in front of the line of police. Then he stopped. There were two lines facing each other, one Stone for one policeman. Angry officials began warning Jeff to move the Stones away from there, they were blocking the sidewalk. "No more'n your fellas," Jeff said. One already sees the outlines of that old psychological shoot-out. The officials threatened Jeff with arrest. Jeff laughed. "Rest me and all my fellas gonna hafta be rested too," and he looked significantly toward the scene of as many Stones as police. For good measure he added, "What we doin' wrong you not doin'?"

He had no idea of going into City Hall. He hadn't been invited to tea with the mayor. The police had shown off a little muscle so he showed off a little muscle. It was, according to the older brothers, utterly useless and a political irrelevance, guaranteed to escalate rage against the Stones. It was useless, all right, except to everyone on the plaza under twenty-five, and everyone really poor, and everyone with a big beef against police-as-such. For them it was the most moving incident of the day. "Ain't they *bad.*"

The Stones were hard-headed—the essence of resistance—they wouldn't take the counsel of friends; they wouldn't take the trou-ble to try to repair their terrible image. They couldn't stop being who they were. Neither can the Cook County Democratic Com-mittee stop being what it is, or change. The Black P. Stone Nation did not devise itself in order to be altered at will by enemies or friends. It has an autonomous existence. When the older brothers treated their activity as though it were kid stuff, the Stones let these highly esteemed leaders know that Blackstone is no respecta-ble colored organization, willing to please City Hall just any old time. When black leaders, businessmen, disc jockeys of renown called for their end, the Stones evenly noted their critics' links to regular lotsabucks black-hating Chicago. When the city fathers de-nounced them, the Stones turned off the sound. They were Stone-to-the-bone, hard-headed outlaws.

One of the more distinguished and oldest groups in the Nation calls itself the Outlaw Rangers. So this final fixing of the issue should not be considered sudden. Vicious, untamable, *civilly dead*, "without rights under the law," and relentless in their public fury, "outlaw" perfectly suits Blackstone, their peoples, and their counterparts across —and under—America.

8 The Story of Eight Outlaw Cop-Killers

Detective James A. Alfano, Jr. was shot on Thursday, August 13, 1970. He died from the bullet wounds the following Sunday.

The Trial

Seven Stones stood trial for the murder of James A. Alfano, Jr., and for conspiracy to commit murder of Chicago police officers. The Stones were defended by James Montgomery, Eugene Pincham, Sam Adams, and Leo Holt. They were the last attorneys employed by the Legal Defense Fund of the First Presbyterian Church of Chicago. The Fund had been terminated between the time of the killing and the trial. After twenty-five months, after spending $600,000, it was clear to First Church officials and to the principal source of the money, Charles F. Kettering II, that the courts of Chicago were no fit place to contest repeated police abuse of its powers to arrest and charge. So the trial was the last gasp of a heroic effort before it bubbled down into briny deeps where so many other Chicago efforts to win some justice had already landed. Had $6,000,000 been spent, the result would not have been significantly different. The poor the Fund sought to defend need to be vaulted up into America before they need lawyers.

After a lengthy process a jury was impaneled and opening statements were made. The state's first witness was Caesari Marsh. He had been charged at one time as the defendants were charged but had been granted immunity so that he might testify about the events of August 13. He was a star witness. He was a freely admitted member of the Black P. Stone Nation. His testimony was immediately damaging to six of the defendants, to Lee Jackson (also charged, but a fugitive at the time of the trial), and to six other members of the Nation who had not been charged. His full testimony under direct examination is found in the transcript of the trial proceedings on Tuesday, December 22, and Wednesday, December 23. (I have omitted from the following summary those portions of the transcript which record Marsh's identification of places and objects in photographs and maps.)

The testimony of Caesari Marsh (summarized):

On August 13 Caesari Marsh arrived at the office of a Stone business operation known as "Black Power Starting Now, Inc." This is located on the south side of 67th Street—almost directly across the street from a storefront which the Stones used as a "center." He arrived in the late morning or early afternoon. He saw defendants Tony Carter, Lamar Bell, Edward Bey, Lee Jackson, Dennis Griffin, Elton Wicks, Ronald Florence, and two other members of the Nation in front of the office. Marsh heard Bell "stating to a group out there that he was tired of officers of the Gang Intelligence Unit Force, Commander Smitty, coming through the neighborhood, jumping on us, fucking with us all the time, and that Smitty and them was going to die that night. And he told us if anybody out there in the crowd planned to be out there later on, he better go home because the lights would be cut off."

Marsh said Edward Bey then told Tony Carter "to get someone to help put the lights out at 67th and Blackstone, and to go down to 63rd Street and tell them to set up some sort of ambush down there so that if the Gang Intelligence Unit officers came through there first they should not reach 67th Street." Leon Witherspoon and David Harshfield (not defendants) were given responsibility to take care of everything at 63rd Street.

Later that afternoon Marsh went into the center and conversed with all of the defendants except William Throop. Six other Stones were in the conversation. He saw Tony Carter bring a rifle into the center. In the conversation, "[Edward] Bey told Carter, after he had the lights put out and everything, to have two men around on the side, set up on the ground, and one man on the roof. Lee Jackson said that all three men should be on the roof so that if they hid from that position, that the police would not know where the fire was coming from."

At 5:30 to 6 P.M. Marsh met Ronald Florence and Tony Carter. Florence said, "Let's get Garry Johnson so we can put the lights out." Florence, Johnson, and Carter went to Bill's car, which was parked nearby. Carter opened the trunk and got a jack handle. While the others acted as lookouts Carter pried open the electricity box which controlled the street lights. Then he went across the street and stuck his hand in the fuse box. Then they all went into the alley—one-half block north on Blackstone Avenue. "There was a piece of a couch and a piece of a chair by this abandoned car and Carter dragged it over by the lamp post and stood up on top of it to go in the fuse box which was not too far off the ground, on the post. He stood up on the piece of couch and opened the box up, went up in the box, put his hand up in there and then after he said it was finished, put the hook back in the box and got back down."

Sometime shortly after 9 P.M. Marsh met with all the defendants (except William Throop). "Carter had a rifle with him. I had a .38 now, Wicks had a .32 automatic, Griffin had a .9 mm automatic, Bell had a .32 five-shot revolver." At about 10:45 "Lee Jackson told us for none of us to get busted with these pieces because there wasn't any bond money, that the chief was gone. Bey said he was going home so if the man rolled down he would be at the crib and if they picked him up they couldn't charge him with anything. . . . Lamar Bell said he was going down to 63rd and help them get the police if they come through there." Marsh then left this grouping on the corner of 67th and Blackstone.

Marsh—with Wicks, Griffin, Carter, and Florence—went to the alley one-half block north. A garage occupies the southeast corner of

Blackstone and the alley. "Carter said somebody should get up on the roof and so Griffin told him that he was going to get up there and he got on the roof and Wicks got behind the bench, and Carter, and Florence, and myself went across the street from there (to the apartment building on the northeast corner of the same intersection— hence directly across from the garage. This building is not located directly at the corner. A small backyard separates it from the alley.) Carter went to the basement. Florence was inside the building. He let Marsh in through the front door. Marsh went to the second floor, walked through the hall to the second-floor back porch. He could hear talking beneath him in the entrance to the basement. He walked inside the house. Then the shooting started. "I heard a loud shot and a bunch of repeated small shots." He came back onto the porch. "I had my gun in my hand and I looked across the street where Griffin and Wicks was positioned and Griffin was standing on the roof, standing up on top of the roof, shooting down at the west portion of the alley."

Marsh ran into the building, got a lady to carry his gun, and the two of them went to a bar next to the center—called McGowan's. He gave the gun to McGowan. He went onto 67th Street. He saw "lots" of police cars and officers by a cleaning shop located on the same north side of 67th Street between Blackstone and the Southmoor Hotel. Bey saw a policeman in a telephone booth and told "Griffin to tell Carter to get the rifle and hit the policeman in the telephone booth." Shortly after, Marsh retrieved his gun from McGowan's and walked back up to the alley. "I saw about nine police officers and a few cars. I looked around behind me to see if anyone was on the street or in the area where I was and when I saw there wasn't anyone there I shot five times down the alley at the police officers who was in the alley." Finally, he hid his gun in an apartment on the north side of 67th Street near Blackstone.

So that is his story. It seemed airtight. It is plausible, full of convincing detail, and fits like a glove with the intimations of super-Blackstone teror which had been sounding in the pretrial publicity. But then Caesari Marsh could not get off the stand and return to his favored witness quarters in the Cook County Jail, not just yet. There was still the formality of cross-examination to be gone through. At the completeion of Marsh's direct examination, Gang Intelligence Unit detectives were exultant and headed off for a few quick ones, as though they were in Wrigley Field at half time and the Bears were ahead, twenty-eight zip.

And now a summary of the cross-examination of Caesari Marsh:

Marsh's direct examination was not the first or only statement he had made about the events of August 13. It was the first one he had made under oath in a courtroom. He had made a sworn statement on the night of August 29, completed early in the morning of August 30. This statement had been made to Lieut. Riley of the Gang Intelligence Unit. Directly after that he made a one-page statement to Lieut. Riley joined by Assistant State's Attorney James Meltreger. Directly after that statement, he made a twenty-four page statement to Meltreger. Marsh was sent to Detroit by the state's attorney's office but did not stay. He returned to Chicago and went to see James Montgomery in his law office. He made a statement there, specifying numerous acts of police brutality practiced on Stones following the shooting. And on November 5 Marsh made yet another statement to Meltreger.

Montgomery and Eugene Pincham tediously developed the complicated history of these statements. One by one the prosecution was forced to hand over the statements to the defense. As the statements became available for scrutiny, numerous discrepancies began to appear. They were right there in the statements. Marsh had no alternative. He had to admit them. Then Montgomery ripped off Mr. Marsh.

Q. You mean you don't know what you said, but yet some of it was true and some of it wasn't?
A. Right.
Q. That's right, is that right?
A. Yes, sir.
Q. So that, even though you do not know what you said, knowing yourself, some of it was true and some was false, is that right?
A. Yes, sir.
Q. That's because, when you rap, you lie sometimes and you tell the truth sometimes, is that right?

A. Yes, sir.

Q. You're rapping now, aren't you?

A. Yes, sir.

Q. You were rapping on the 23rd, weren't you?

A. Yes, sir.

Q. You were rapping to the jury on the 22nd, weren't you?

A. Yes, sir.

Q. You are still rapping, right?

A. Yes.

The witness had discredited his own testimony. Marsh admitted he had lied to the jury. Furthermore, he admitted he had lied in his previous statements. The defense did not arrest the cross-examination after forcing such a damaging admission. It sought to discover the meaning of the lies by investigating each discrepancy. The cross-examination was long and vigorous. These points emerged:

1. The first statement referred to a shooting in the alley behind *1520* East 67th Street. This was at least fifty feet east of where trial testimony placed it. Accordingly, the first statement, made on August 29–30, made no mention of a couch being dragged to a lamppost. Marsh said Carter got a *ladder* from Bill's car. Once the shooting had been shifted to the west end of the alley a couch was required to furnish Carter the means to reach the fuse box and to obstruct the police car. Or perhaps it was the other way around; an obstruction was required. How can the place of shooting just jump around like that?

2. In his first statement on August 29–30 Marsh did not mention being on the second-floor back porch of the apartment building; he did not state he was carrying a .38 revolver. That statement had Marsh on the corner of 67th and Blackstone at the time of the shooting. From that vantage point he "saw" the squad car racing across Blackstone after the loud shot. How could a witness, who really saw the events, and really remembered them, almost casually testify to critically different versions?

3. Elton Wicks had been named by Marsh in the first statement as the man who had the rifle. And according to that statement, Wicks

was in the basement doorway of the apartment building; Dennis
Griffin was on the roof of the garage. Ronald Florence wasn't even
mentioned. But Marsh had told the jury that Tony Carter had the
rifle; Elton Wicks was on the garaage roof; Ronald Florence had been
given a role. Since the testimony in all statements deals with one rifle,
it is difficult to suppose first one man and then another had it—
particularly difficult when the testimony does not present a rifle being
shifted back and forth like the shooting site. In each statement someone had the rifle all the way through the evening. But who?

4. The first statement contains no reference to Edward Bey's order
to shoot a policeman in the telephone booth and is silent about Marsh
firing five shots at the policemen.

5. The fourth statement had been given to James Montgomery
outside the presence of the police and without their consent. The
defense used that as a road map to where the other statcmets were
located in the landscape of shifting shooting scenarios. Testifying
about the fourth statement—on the stand, remember—Marsh admitted that before Lieut. Riley took his first statement, he invited Marsh
to give a hand-written statement. Marsh wrote out such a statement,
but Lieut. Riley did not like it. He accused Marsh of lying and tore
it up. After that he *and* Lieut. Riley prepared the statement identified
above as the *first* statement. But now, revelations within revelations,
James Meltreger appeared on the scene of this statement preparation.

Q. During that time he told you that he had read the statement which is
Defendant's S-1 [the first statement], which you have previously given and
signed, didn't he?
A. Yes.
Q. And he told you that that was not an accurate statement, didn't he?
A. That is correct.
Q. And after he told you that, it was then that Defendant's Exhibit Number
S-2, for identification, was prepared, isn't that right?
A. That is correct.

The last answer was given over the strenuous objections of the prosecution. But the judge allowed it to be made. Suddenly the smooth S-2

became suspect with its many questions and answers, all stenographically recorded and full of careful lawyer talk.

6. The defense finally got to the heart of the case: Who pulled the trigger? Neither the murder charges nor the conspiracy charges could be sustained without hard evidence that some *one* pulled the trigger or without similarly hard evidence that some one of a finite set of conspiring suspects had pulled the trigger. Here the star witness has got to be believable. Realizing that they might actually have a chance to *win* this case, the defense really went after Caesari Marsh. Mr. Pincham was the cross-examiner.

Q. In S-1 you say you saw a man with a rifle run out of the alley into Blackstone and shoot as the squad car went west to the alley, is that right?
A. That is correct.
Q. Now, before the Court and ladies and gentlemen of the jury you said you didn't see the man with the rifle shot, is that correct?
A. That is correct.
Q. Then in S-3 when you were talking to Meltreger you told him the man came out of the alley, put a rifle to his shoulder and fired, is that right?
A. That is correct.
Q. That was a lie, wasn't it?
A. Yes.
Q. When in S-5 you told Meltreger that you didn't see the man with the rifle shoot but you heard him shoot underneath where you were, that is in the basement stairwell in the building on the corner, is that right?
A. That is correct.

These admissions were crucial. A witness would have to be imbecilic or pathological to swear to such grossly conflicting memories of an event. Just because Caesari Marsh was a good-looking and very bright young man the defense had narrowed the possible explanations of his conflicting testimonies to one: he had altered his memory on purpose. The alterations furnish clues to the purpose involved.

On August 29–30 the purpose was to have a star witness identify a man running into Blackstone Avenue, putting a rifle to his shoulder, and firing at a squad car as it went west. After Meltreger entered, the purpose shifted. The Meltreger-Marsh purpose then was to have a star witness identify a man running into the alley and firing a rifle. But on November 5 the purpose had shifted again. It was: to have a star witness identify a man in a basement stairwell with a rifle, then remember hearing a rifle shot.

Even a jury should be able to figure that one out. For a while the state was intending to charge one of the defendants specifically with the murder; then it decided not to. Instead, it decided to charge none specifically but all collectively with shooting the lethal shot. The reason for lying became more important than the lying itself. The witness's memory was no longer the point. The exigencies of prosecution had taken over. The spotlight shifted from rotten lying witness to the scheming Meltreger in the wings, guiding the words of his hapless puppet witness, for which favor, or course, the witness had been excused from trial on these very charges, and his family had received hundreds of dollars—as he also admitted, truthfully.

Next, the testimony of police officers in summary:

Officers Thomas Donahue and Richard Crowley were in the unmarked police car on August 13 when their fellow officer, James Alfano, was shot. Their testimony was similar, free of inconsistencies, and was received by the defense attorneys with very little objection. The cross-examination was almost perfunctory. Their testimony: the car entered the north-south alley behind the Southmoor Hotel from 67th Street, hence was traveling north. The car proceeded past the east-west alley which dead-ends at the alley behind the hotel. But the car couldn't go all the way through the north-south alley because a road-block-type obstruction was in the way. Officer Crowley was at the wheel. He backed the car up and started west in the east-west alley. Another obstruction appeared. A couch was partially blocking the alley. Just as the driver began to move the couch aside with the front bumper and left front fender of the car, one loud rifle shot was heard, followed by what sounded like small-arms fire. Alfano said he had been hit. The driver then sped to Billings Hospital.

Officer John Degnan and Officer Willie Anderson, in separate cars and different locations, heard the radio alarm and drove immediately to the scene of the shooting. They parked their cars and joined other police officers by then on the scene. They both testified that the area was dark. Only one street light was burning—where the two alleys intersected. (Officers Donahue and Crowley also specifically remembered the solitary street light.) The officers in the area received small-arms fire from the western darkness of the east-west alley. The police took cover and did not return fire. After the ranking officer on the scene dismissed Degnan and Anderson, they returned to their regular duties.

So far so good. The prosecution was quickly repairing the damage done them by Caesari Marsh. Suddenly the defense stopped being perfunctory and aggressively cross-examined Willie Anderson. Now, what about that street light? Where was it exactly? Officer Anderson knew exactly where it was: on a utility pole located at the southwest corner of the intersection of the alleys. Was there any chance he might have confused this utility pole with some other one? Well, Officer Anderson knew there was no other pole in the vicinity, how could he confuse it with nothing?

Attorney Pincham dramatically asked for police photographs of the shooting scene taken on August 14 and admitted previously into evicence by the state. He brought the photographs over to the loyal officer and asked him to point out the street light. A silence followed as the witness stared at the photographs. The silence gathered and was more eloquent than the witness's eventual admission that the photographs did not show that there was a street light on that utility pole. Mr. Pincham then introduced some recent pictures of the scene as defense exhibits. The witness was asked to point out the street light on the utility pole. He couldn't. It wasn't there then any more than it had been there on the day after the shooting.

The defense was mindful of public reluctance to admit that police officers can fail to remember all items of evidence on the witness stand, so after driving Anderson to the point where he had to admit his uncertainty, they relented. They were not after Willie Anderson, a brother. They were after James Meltreger.

To prove his case, Meltreger needed the lights turned off down the alley so he could have a couch there so he could have conspirators in a nearby stairwell. He needed a single street light illuminating the gathered police officers at the *(real)* scene, namely, at the intersection of the alleys (why else were they all down there instead of where the couch was?), so that they could be fired upon, and so that another witness could see the first obstruction being built earlier in the evening.

The defense made a big to-do about Willie Anderson's report of the August 13 events. The report showed on its face that it had been filed December 13, fully two weeks after the trial had begun. The judge had no alternative. He impounded all prosecution files to prohibit the prosecution from supplementing those files with predated reports. He struggled against having to do it but he knew he had to; otherwise appellate review would throw the whole trial out.

And now, a summary of the Testimony of Ernest Williams:

Ernest Williams is an eighteen-year-old young man who lives in Woodlawn. He was seen in the area of the shooting on the night of the crime. He testified that had been a member of the Black P. Stone Nation. On the night of August 13 he was walking past the north end of the north-south alley and saw Tony Carter, Edward Bey, Lee Jackson, and William Throop. The first three were pushing a large couch into a lot of debris already piled in the alley. It looked like a roadblock. William Throop was standing by with a rifle. He could see these people well enough to identify them in an otherwise darkened alley because a single street light was burning at the intersection of the alleys.

This wasn't the first time Ernest Williams had testified, either. He had testified before the grand jury and the earlier testimony did not agree with the testimony he had just given. Under the pressure of cross-examination he admitted adding to and subtracting from his earier testimony after talking to James Meltreger. He was impeaching himself right along and could no more evade the missing street light than Anderson when that subject was brought up. What remained was to tie Meltreger into the testimonies:

Q. And the first time you said anything about any trash being in the alley was after you talked to Meltreger, isn't that right?

A. Yes.

Q. Well, the first time that you said that you saw somebody in the alley pushing a couch toward a pile of trash was when you were talking to James Meltreger, is that not correct, sir?

A. This is correct.

Scratch Ernest Williams.

And on to the Testimony of Rose Wilkins:

Mrs. Wilkins is a long-time resident of the immediate neighborhood. She testified that on the night of August 13 William Throop and Edward Bey had warned her that there was going to be shooting and counseled her to go inside her house and stay inside. She said she had known both young men for many years. She was asked to point them out in the courtroom—a routine procedure scarcely necessary in light of her long-time acquaintance. Well, she misidentified one and could not find the second at all. So much for Rose Wilkins. Judge Garippo instructed the jury thereupon to disregard her testimony.

In summary:

Without intending it, the prosecution had succeeded in raising a lot of questions. An immediate question is raised by the failure of the state to seek to corroborate some of the testimony. The lady who carried Caesari Marsh's pistol for him could have been brought in to support his story. Someone in McGowan's could have confirmed receiving and holding the gun. Someone from the Bureau of Electricity could have sworn the fuse boxes had been tampered with on August 13. If they had, someone would have had to restore them to working order sometime. When corroboration lies so close at hand, almost suggesting itself, and it is not offered, it maybe does not exist. Perhaps the darkened alley came out of Meltreger's game plan.

Ernest Williams and Caesari Marsh, even in their un-cross-examined testimonies, conflict with each other. Since neither could be correct without attacking the testimony of the other, the question effortlessly arises: Was neither correct?

The main question, however, is the shooting site. One can see why the prosecution-police-state's attorney team wanted it further and further west in the alley until it finally was placed almost to Blackstone Avenue. Yet this is thrown into absolute question by the testimony of Officer Crowley. He swore that after hearing Alfano was shot he took off. He was going so fast by the time he reached Blackstone (one-way south) that it would have been unsafe to make that left turn, so he kept on across Blackstone in the alley all the way to the next street before turning left down to 67th Stteet. Do you see? If he had started up only twenty-five feet away from Blackstone Avenue, there is no way he could have accelerated to thirty-five to forty m.p.h. by the time he got there. No way, not even in a Mercedes 300 SEL. Why did the state want to shift the site? What went on down there so unpleasant to their case? To get blunt about it, what did they want to hide?

Associated with the site question is the trigger-man question. About the only defendant not seen by somebody somewhere in the prosecution's case with the rifle was Lamar Bell—the Stone identified to Judge Hechinger in a pre-trial arraignment as the trigger man. The lethal bullet passed through the trunk of the squad car on almost level flight, which is an impossible shot from a stairwell just a little ahead of the car when the shot was fired. Did the prosecution intend the jury to help themselves to some potluck speculation about how the guy in the stairwell—to be named finally by the jury—got the bullet through the trunk and fatally into Alfano?

The Defense Non-Case. Since none of the defendants would have testified if their attorneys had required them to, it was just as well that the defense team could argue that reasonable doubts had been raised already and they had no need to waste everybody's time.

Caesari Marsh's Redirect Examination. The prosecution sought to rehabilitate its star witness. He came back onto the stand and testified that he had placed a long-distance telephone call to James Montgomery on Sunday morning, September 4. Montgomery received the collect call from the office of "Black Power Starting Now, Inc." Marsh had made the call, he swore, because his chief, Jeff Fort, had ordered him to—in accordance with an order to lie to the police. Had Jeff Fort also ordered him to lie to the judge and jury? You bet.

Under its redirect cross-esamination of Caesari Marsh, the defense did finally call some witnesses of its own. An employee of the telephone company testified that there was no record of the Detroit– "Black Power Starting Now, Inc." telephone call on that Sunday morning, or any other time. The next witness testified that James Montgomery was fishing in Indiana the whole Sunday morning of September 4. The attempt to rehabilitate Caesari Marsh ended in disaster.

The Verdicts

The transcript leads to one conclusion. Judge Louis Garippo should have directed not Guilty verdicts after the Marsh testimony, or, failing that, certainly after the Anderson testimony, or, at the absolute latest, after the state rested its case. No mere "reasonable" doubt had been raised. Something close to indismissible doubt of absolute proportions had been raised. In light of that failure of the judge's nerve, it should not have required a jury more than ten minutes to vote Not Guilty verdicts all the way around.

The transcript is misleading; it records only what was *said* in the trial. It takes no account of how people in the courtroom—especially the defendants, in this case—looked, and how they acted, and what impressions they made on the jury. The Stones themselves, just by sitting there all supercool, square-jawed, displaying their rotten attitude toward the whole thing, were undoing the work of their attorneys and rebuilding the state's case as fast as it got torn down. Their reputation preceded their presence, of course, and the two combined to suggest something between menace and terror. They looked guilty.

So the jury stayed out a lot longer than ten minutes. It stayed out three days. There was no doubt about how they would vote. The difficulty was supposed to be a reluctant juror or two. They would soon see the light. But the certainty of straight Guilty verdicts began to wane the longer the jury stayed out. The jury was supposed to be compromising in order to find some defendants guilty and some not guilty. When the jury remained out, the certainty was that some would be guilty of the murder, others of the conspiracy charge. Speculation of this nature went on among professional and layman alike, unable to handle anything but guilty-type outcomes.

When the jury announced it was finished, Judge Garippo had to be summoned from a Black Hawks hockey game. Attorneys from both sides were similarly informed and came running from their various Sunday afternoons. The defendants, of course, were brought over from the Cook County Jail.

To the astonishement of everyone, including Justice, who is alleged to have lifted her blindfold to assure herself she was hearing right, the jury declared the outlaw Stones Not Guilty. The jury was a bold bunch to have stuck to a study of the evidence or, rather, the nonevidence.

Before joining in the singing of a stanza or two from the "Star Spangled Banner," this American system of justice, which seemed to have shown itself off to pretty good effect in the Alfano trial, deserves to be thought about a bit longer.

What went wrong in the state's rush to get these particular defendants into the chair or, at least, into the penitentiary for life? Obviously the defense got in the way. The state had not figured on a team of bright and aggressive defense attorneys with a lot of experience in the criminal courts, who thus know about "statements," and star witnesses, and corrigible police officers. Throughout the latter stages of the trial the prosecution attorneys wore expressions of pained disbelief. They considered it an affront that the defense was defending. They were occasionally outraged, too, at the unorthodox (black) dialogues going on between *their* witnesses and the defense attorneys. (The prosecution blew up over the repeated use of such an unheard-of and imprecise term as "rapping.") The brilliant defense pointed out that something was wrong; *they* weren't the wrong. What was wrong with the state's case began going wrong fifteen minutes after the shooting and continued to go wrong as the police contributed their peculiar "information" to the case.

The police work done by the Gang Intelligence Unit was what was wrong or, more accurately said, was not done. It was inept, as Meltreger's preparation was pitiful. As the matter is pondered, this colossal ineptitude is neither a function of stupidity nor of shoddiness, although both are in abundant evidence throughout the transcript. The ineptitude seems to be a function of something more sinsister, like arrogance. After coming to a lightning conclusion about who did it, the police set about constructing a case which would sustain their conclusion. They did what they knew to do. They put pressure on suspects and after getting one to turn their way, they placed their story in his mouth. It did not occur to the police to look at real things such as utility poles or acceleration tables. They arrogantly assumed that their power to arrest and formulate charges extended onto reality itself. They looked upon the trial as the occasion for the vindication of their presentation of reality, and definitely not as adversarial proceedings designed to flush out all lurking truth.

Perhaps use of the strong word "arrogance" is misleading; it is too psychologically pointed, as if to locate the wrong in police feelings. Let them feel what they will, the wrong is located in their contempt of the law and this shows up in their procedures, not their feelings.

The Stones certainly sang no "Star Spangled Banner" in thankfulness for the jury system after the Alfano trial. They found no reason to be grateful. They *already* knew it was a fluke. Procedures are more powerful than juries. As if to prove the Stones right, the police and the state attorney's office, shortly after the verdicts were in, said they were closing the case. They believed they had got the right guys but the wrong jury. So who did kill Alfano? The Stones *already* knew such a question would not occur to the police. The civilly dead did it, the outlaw Stones.

9   The Briarpatch

The opposite of *outlaw* is *straight*. This scale replaces previous scales such as guilty/not guilty, criminal/clean, Democratic/Republican, black/white, rich/poor/subpoor, friend/foe. The terms of the new scale define each other. To be *outlaw* means to be relentless untamable enemy of straight society, what earlier was called regular America. To be *straight* means to honor the conventions of straight society which are threatened and come into view only when threatened by outlaws. Straight people only find out about the conventions of regular work done by regular people when a horde of maniacs rip into a building project where regular work is going on. Then straight people know the difference between themselves and outlaws. Outlaws most always are violent. This means they do violent deeds (they shoot policemen) and they might do violent deeds (they might shoot policemen). *Straight,* then, also means peaceful, while *outlaw* means violent.

The outlaws would not abide the conventions. They broke out of their jail and came violently right into the living middle of the straight world. They would not stay in their psychological jail: the subghetto. They tore it down, as they earlier promised they would. "Let us outa this goddamn jail or we tear it down." They had to screw up their deal, as they had the St. Charles rehabilitation before. They also ripped off Mayor Daley himself with that no-voting prank of theirs. Their gall seems unlimited.

One must not assume *outlaw* is a specially devised way to discuss the Black P. Stone Nation. They are but the leaders of the gang of outlaws which numbers, well, that is the fear, because who knows how many there are? Who has ever bothered to notice them, much less to count them? They are out there, nonetheless, malingering, bilking welfare, shooting up dope or hopped up with some crazy superspeed, ready to retch all over the first counter to shove his head in the door, or poke him in the nose. Blackstone is just their very tough representative. Definitions which call them sub-American, subpoor, subblack are not quite adequate because the prefixes in the definitions seem to stand for a hope and could present a challenge to some Americans to try to erase them. The situation is a lot better defined with *outlaw,* because it comprehends their hell-no perfectly and, of course, the straight response of horror.

These people in some out-there, Stone peoples one and all, are what make the Stones appear so dangerous to straight society. The peoples have already shown dangerous tendencies on their own. As has earlier been remarked, they sometimes go wild and burn their communities, rob merchants clean, shoot at approaching firemen and the police, fight arresting officers, and curse the judge who sentences them. The actual Stone peoples—on Chicago's south side—are more dangerous than that because they have not done the wild stuff—yet. They are apparently better controlled, more disciplined, waiting for the right time to pull off *their* conflagration. It is certain they are capable of it. That certainty is heightened by the presence of Blackstone among them. Was it not their great strength among the peoples which the Stones demonstrated, and wasn't this the very thing which provoked the final showdown?

This is a point of considerable importance. Outlaw means all of those people, not just leaders of special outlaw organizations. The peoples-outlaws are that whole rotting-away, mad, beaten-up bunch of cast-offs. They are an incredible bunch which can even ruin elections. Now one begins to understand how startling Jeff's words were to the princes. "We gonna have our own govament," he said, "the way our daddies did long time back. And what peoples git messed up by the polices and such is gonna be our peoples. They don't let us in their govament, we git our own. They not let us in, we be OUT." The authorities would have been well advised to have studied their Sartre a little more carefully. He would have told them they were embarking on an unproductive course in dealing with these Stone peoples. "They sometimes organize among themselves, educate themselves and become conscious of their race or class. They then discover, through hatred, the meaning of reciprocity, and the oppressor comes to personify Evil for them just as they personify Evil for the oppressor."* It is a short step from out to outlaw to outlaw nation, constituted of those who despise the other nation, its ways, and its authorities. Is this a black separatism, registered perhaps in a different key, and unadorned with Muslim embellishments? It doesn't appear to be. It seems more like a way to mess up the Man's game and see what happens next. Straight organizations have goals, including black separatist organizations. Outlaws "see what's gonna happen," going along from day to day, ad hoc, unpredictable. One never knows about them.

Driving slowly through Jackson Park on a blistering-hot summer night, one might hear the brothers in the dark with their bongos. It seems they are sounding out a "We Shall Overcome," but the beat appears to be 5/4 and the notes of the lightly voiced melody are coming out at an astonishing rate, considering the tune is so often heard at medium-slow tempos. The brothers are overcoming the beat and the accents of "We Shall Overcome." This seems to be a jungle music—surely not Bossa Nova or Island rhythms—suited to young men who appreciate the difference between a .357 magnum and a spear. It is very dangerous stuff one hears out in the dark where the difference between Stone and non-Stone cannot be observed. They are *all* dangerous, overcoming the "overcomers"—who overcame them —and getting ready for who knows what new stunt.

The country and Chicago have finally caught up to where First Church was when it began its association with Blackstone. The church recognized Blackstone as a power organization in itself which

*Saint Genet (New York: George Braziller, 1963), pp. 30, 31.

also represented the power of a vastly greater population of ghetto youth, children, and the cast-offs. The children could be heard happily singing, "Mighty, mighty Blackstone," as they played in the streets. The church devoted its life to the support of Blackstone's existence as a power organization, which included, of course, the perpetual possibliity the south side might be blown up at any minute. While fully aware of Blackstone's outlaw stance, the church did not insist, as the rest of the country now has, that they be clapped into jail. Quite the contrary, the church agreed with Blackstone on the fundamental matter of that black nation. That was the ticket. Thus when the church was variously accused of contributing to the formation of a black Mafia, a black octopus, thereby hastening the destruction of the community, the church responded with a hearty, "Nonsense!" leaving unsaid the remaining, "We have no interest in black Mafias. We are interested in Blackstone's idea of a whole *nation,* starting from 21st Street and running to 250th Street, every outcast black man, woman, and child welded into a unity of willfulness and rage. It sounds a good bit like an empire to us, and that's what is needed."

We were, of course, mad. Nothing else explains our condition. We were afflicted with lunacy, forgetting cool cynicism and good sense. It was much like Nessim's famous revelations to Justine in Durrell's *Mountolive.* An absolutely startling idea had forged the association. "All of the black people from 21st Street to 250th Street welded into a unity of . . ."; but should it happen, that would be the ball game, wouldn't it? There would for absolute sure be some freedom and justice around the place. And the genius of the idea occurs in its origin, not its shape. The peoples would be in the position to get what straight society had denied and withheld.

The straight society does not so positively cheer the possibility of a black empire stretching even one block, from 21st Street to 22nd Street, to say nothing of "all the way to 250th Street." It fears the idea of a nation or an empire or even an organization of the outlaws and has mounted an enormous engine of destruction to prohibit its formation. Straight wants *one* nation under God, not two, but apparently is willing to finesse the "liberty and justice for all," or allow it to mean "for all straights."

Outlaw is not a word too often encountered. Its synonyms, however, have become almost household expressions. They are: black militants, black revolutionaries, black-power advocates, members of radical groups, black radicals, black anarchists, black communists, Black Panthers, Blackstone Rangers, Revolutionary Action Movement, Mau-Maus, and black activitists. An outlaw is an identified enemy of straight society. He is not much to be found walking around on the streets, therefore. He is, instead, in one of three places. He is in jail; he is in hiding; he is in exile. He admits he is an enemy of straight society; so, more than incorrigible, he is relentlessly and vociferously incorrigible. Since he will not stay in the conventional psychological jail, he must be hounded out of his hiding place and put behind the safety of real bars. And should any other outlaws become daring enough to identify themselves, they may expect the same going to jail.

An outlaw chief, Jeff Fort, failed to appear at a hearing in one of his many pending cases. In September of 1970 he had been variously charged with attempted murder, murder, kidnaping, aggravated assault, contempt of Congress, fraud, conspiracy to commit fraud, mob action, and disorderly conduct, all of which existed as a series of cases coming up. He had heard from sources he trusted that a brand-new warrant would be waiting for him when he showed up at the particular hearing in September. This warrant, he was warned, would be the clincher, the one to get him in jail finally, out of reach of further bail, further legal defense, and further exercise of the "liberty" to walk around. So he decided he wouldn't appear at that or at the further hearings which kept coming up. One by one his bail bonds fell, and, one by one, bail-jumping charges were added to the existing charges. He was a fugitive from federal and Cook County justice, and really not caring much, since showing up or not showing up at various courthouses did not alter the determination of the authorities to bring him into their jail forever or his determination to resist them.

His friends said he was in Detroit, in Cleveland, in Los Angeles, back in Detroit. However that may be, he kept appearing in Woodlawn to counsel with Stone leaders. Friends also said he was in and out of Canada in preacher's clothes, a vigorous young black prelate going to dinner in Windsor after a hard day saving souls in some Detroit parish. Friends also said he was going to have a "boss rap" with Kenyatta, and had the visa, passport, and papers ready to go, as a fake clergyman, real fugitive, and monster outlaw all at once.

Friends are not always reliable since they cannot bear to say they do not know. One simply does not know about Jeff Fort. He was in Woodlawn all right, for he had been definitely seen walking down the street one afternoon at two o'clock. And he left Woodlawn, all right, in the company of Chester Evans and they went to New York, and they had airplane tickets to Toronto, as well as papers to get them to a more friendly country, although the newspapers do not reveal which one. If it was his intention to go into exile, he waited too long. A girl aroused the suspicions of the G.I.U. They followed the girl to New York, from the Kennedy International Airport, to the St. George Hotel, and in the company of some of New York's finest entered, finally, the lair of the outlaw chief.

So he was caught and brought back to the Cook County jail, from which he periodically issues to stand yet another trial, ending in Not Guilty or hung jury. But never mind, he will be there a long time because the cases against him are inexhaustible. At one particular time in the fall of 1970 there were nineteen fellow Stone chiefs in the same jail along with Jeff Fort, each one with some series of charges backed up against him, perhaps eligible for bond, probably not. The other chiefs come and go. Jeff goes on forever. And Gene Hairston sits grinding his teeth in the downstate Illinois penitentiary at Menard, knowing he will not be paroled, planning to come back out in 1973, having begun his "time" in 1968 for a crime the G.I.U. should know was committed by someone else.

Outlaws differ from straights in almost all particulars. But the central difference has come to be that outlaws are in jail, or will be put in jail as soon as they can be found. They are all wanted. While it seems as if the authorities are determined to break up organizations such as the Black Panthers, the Black P. Stone Nation, R.A.M., the Blood Brothers, and a thousand similar organizations stirring to life in the alleyways of metropolitan America, that is no longer the dominant intention. Purpose has been refined by experience. The intention is to get all of the identified outlaws into jail the minute they declare themselves and can be rounded up.

It is stunning bad politics on the part of the authorities to jail outlaws, if it is their official intention to keep their jails safe for democracy. The one place in Chicago with the highest concentration of incendiary wrath would appear to rational men to be the one place the popular band of Stone charismatics should be banned from, at all costs. Surely they haven't forgotten to do what they learned to do right there. It seems the authorities are playing a game of touch football on top of a nitroglycerin factory. With Stone hotshots in jail, not the run-of-the-mill outlaws but the very most talented organizers in the Nation, the issues are not going to languish, or resistance either. They have an uncanny way of making believers out of outcasts, "Put some Stone in their black heads." And they have the capacity to get the fires of resistance stoked up so high the very lids on the jail might blow off.

Might blow off? What would one call the events in Joliet, Pontiac, and Cook County jails in the last year? They are "Stone jails" every one. They differ in no important respect from Attica, San Quentin, Folsom, Soledad. The outlaws seem to be having a resistance blast in jail no matter where they are. They are not wasting any time. In fact they have changed the meaning of "doing time." Worried prison officials, governors, prestigious investigating groups have now begun to sound a small alarm of indignation that society's problems have been cast into jail. One day their complaint will be virtually identical with that of police officers who now are worried about going into the ghettos for fear of being sniped. Well, the outlaws can't be kept in jail forever. One day they will have to be released to the street, if only to preserve the jails. When they return to the streets they will not have been exactly mollified by their jail experience. It seems likely they will be twice as mad and more determined than ever to continue their resistance stuff on and on.

Jail is the outlaw's briarpatch. He neither disappears nor dies when he goes to jail. He continues on as does the issue which is absolutely primary to these lower-than-poor and abused sub-Americans. It simply will not go away.

Hannah Arendt, in her clear, persuasive account of the difference between violence and power remarks on the fading power of the police and believes extensive resort to violence demonstrates how clearly they know it. Already bad authorities do not become better by becoming more violent. They become worse authorities and lose more power in the act. Furthermore, she entertains few hopes for the reauthentication of power through licit civilized procedures in mass societies. She focuses attention particularly on the authoritylessness of bureaucracies. No one is minding the store, she says, neither the representatives of the people nor the people. No one likes it, but no one, either, has a mandate to do something about it. "We know," she writes, "or should know, that every decrease in power is an open invitation to violence—if only because those who hold power and feel it slipping away from their hands, be they the government or be they the governed, have always found it difficult to resist the temptation to substitute violence for it."*

She opens the violence matter in a realistic way. Confrontations between the authorities and hostile Stone peoples seemingly show on their face a discrepancy between power on the side of the police and powerlessness on the side of the people. Arendt's analysis strips away that face. Were the police genuinely powerful and were they actual authorities, they would not be in a confrontation, and definitely would not be indulging in adolescent games. Similarly, Stone peoples would not be taunted into violence as some kind of urgent rebuttal, or initiate violence later as an afterthought to rebuttal.

The construction of the primary issue along a straight/outlaw series is preposterous. It invites the violence which invoked it. That the violence has been placed behind prison walls has not stopped it. It careens the more wildly out of control precisely because the human sensibilities of its users, guard and prisoner alike, are deadened the more this violence comes at them. Arendt's point is, recall, that no

*On Violence (New York: Harcourt, Brace & World, Inc., 1969), p. 87.

one is minding the store. The failure to deal with the primary human-social-economic-political issues of subcitizenship (not the "have-nots" surely, but the "never-will-gits"), sliding it over to the police to handle when the police have difficulty in handling themselves, is a failure for which no one is *exactly* responsible. Everyone is. But when said in that way, it means no one is.

Hannah Arendt disclaims knowledge of the future. She refuses to predict what is going to happen. That is a wisdom seldom encountered in one so brilliant. The less wise do not hesitate, however, and have written their scenarios of future events with alacrity, according to which a little violence now, some moderate or benigned neglect of due process will forestall apocalypse, American history in the years 1965–71 notwithstanding. The people standing outside America in 1965 were astonishingly troublesome. Their anger and unutterable poverty were revolting. It was then thought some "good" hard police work would straighten them out. But it didn't. When they didn't relent in their not having and wanting the elementary felicities of civilized life, they were subjected to a sickening wave of sheer brutal violence. They returned with some violence of their own and for their trouble have been jailed and must endure all over again the harsh abuse which provoked their violence. Does it seem rational to suppose this will improve the situation? This little more violence, this moderate neglect of due process will not protect civilized life, surely, but will inevitably degrade it. This makes the hard-liner scenarios of future events, featuring public tranquility and safety for all, especially frightening. They pretend to know too much about the future, in spite of overwhelming evidence that the "knowledge" is already discredited. What then becomes clear is not the future, but the futility of assigning the task of solving the problem to the very people who have done so much to aggravate it.

The future is a mystery. Let us leave it at that. Owing to the endurance of the cast-offs, however, there is still a question written across its face, that very same primordial question no less urgent now for being in the mouths of outlaws: "Are you gonna let everybody born here be real Americans, or only the ones suit you?"

My memoir ends with an acid Stone reminiscence. A Stone was in my office one day, passing the time, and said:

I be seein' these li'l kids, li'l *bitty* kids over round Chuck's house [in Hyde Park]. In the playgrounds, up in there somewhere. So tiny can't hardly walk. You know what I'm sayin'? This one li'l dude I watched. He run all round where his mama is sittin' on a bench. And he be lookin' to see his mama lookin' at him, dig. He laugh and run back to where she is at and she pat 'im on the ass and he run some more. Nother kid be playin' over on the side, kinda. Jest playin' along, mindin' his own business. He run over there and come up from behind and push the other kid over on his face. He's bawlin', raisin' hell, like that. The li'l kid, the one I's talkin' 'bout, he's not lookin' back *now*. He's not lookin' round to see mama lookin' at him. He's runnin' off to play with his trucks. Like nothin' at all be wrong. He don't wanna give his mama the chance to say he's mean, you understand. You know, Fry, those li'l kids got so much toys and trucks and stuff they gotta be number-one mechanics fore they's five years old. Man! All that struttin' round, gittin' their ass patted. They be so full of ME. Lookit ME, Mama. Lookit me practicin' on goin' down to the loop when I git growed up to pick up the big bread. Lookit me practicin' on push the li'l mother on his face. Knocks me plumb out. ME, *I* be hidin' behind cars, duckin' round buildins, lookin' everywheres for peoples *not* to see me. ME practicin' on bein' a ghost, tryin' to stay way from double O buckshot in my head. It ain't right, someway.

After a long ruminative pause he got up, stretched, and as he walked out added, "It's a bullshit scene, Jack."

Appendix

The Famous Raid on the

"Arsenal of the Blackstone Rangers"

An unusual meeting took place in the pastors' study of First Church on June 28, 1966. The meeting was attended by
—representatives of First Church
—representatives of the Grand Crossing Police District
—representatives of the Blackstone Rangers
—representatives of the youth detection unit of the Chicago Police Department
—agents of the Alcohol and Tax Division of the U.S. Treasury Department (charged with enforcing federal statutes prohibiting unlicensed possession and use of automatic weapons, sawed-off weapons, and hand weapons with obliterated serial numbers)
The specific goal of the meeting was to determine possible terms and procedures for a disarmament of the Blackstone Rangers. The difficulties encountered before the meeting, making the meeting necessary, were twofold. First, Blackstone distrusted the law-enforcement officials. Second, law-enforcement officials had failed to accomplish disarmament by use of their normal procedures, such as the detection and apprehension of persons with illegal weapons, and the deterrence to possession and use of prohibited weapons that five-year sentences in a federal penitentiary represented. Rangers and officials had ample reason to work something out. A bargain of sorts emerged in the meeting.

167

The Blackstone Rangers promised to collect and turn in their weapons on or before July 4.

The federal agents promised to intervene in two important pending court cases, scheduled for trial on July 8 and 15 by informing the judges of the result of the gun collection. The agents reported, furthermore, that a federal pressure would be applied against the possession and use of prohibited weapons in the area of the Devil's Disciples commencing on July 5.

The police representatives promised to intervene in the two pending court cases. The police freely admitted that three of the four Rangers charged with illegal possession of a shotgun in the July 15 case were innocent of the charges and every effort would be made to free three of the four. These policemen also promised to add squad cars to the regular nighttime patrols in order to afford additional protection to the disarmed Rangers against possible Disciple raids.

The First Church representatives promised to let the building be used in the gun collection as a neutral collection site. They also consented to a request that their walk-in safe be used for the storage of all weapons collected which did not fall under federal statutory jurisdiction.

The performance of all parties would be reviewed at a meeting to be convened thirty days after the gun collection. If the terms of the agreement were found to have been kept, the guns not falling under federal jurisdiction and stored in the safe would be removed from the safe and turned over to the police.

One must admit at the outset that this was an improbable meeting. But it pleased the participants to have worked out a solution to a complicated set of problems.

A further meeting on July 1 worked out the final details of the gun collection. The collection ended at 9 A.M. on July 4. Rangers voluntarily surrendered numerous assorted weapons. The number cannot be exactly determined, but was in the vicinity of and higher than 100. Agent Pete Zelkovich called it a significant disarmament at the time. He and his colleagues confiscated the weapons they were obliged to pick up. The remainder were inventoried and placed in the walk-in safe. This safe had been used to store valuable historical records and documents. They had been removed. The safe was put to an unintended but highly purposeful use. Once the safe was locked, a copy of the inventory of weapons in the safe was signed by Agent Pete Zelkovich and a representative of the Chicago Police Department. The inventory and the written combination to the walk-in safe were placed in an envelope. It was sealed and stored in the safe which the church regularly uses for the storage of money, valuable papers, and the like. It was known to all parties that only two people in the entire world knew the combination of that safe and of the walk-in safe, two mature women of impeccable character: Miss Geraldine Eggers, the church's program director, and Mrs. Emmanuel Jones, the financial secretary.

On July 8 the first case came up and was continued. On July 15 the second—shotgun—case came up and was continued. But inasmuch as Eugene Hairston had been (erroneously) charged with illegal possession of the shotgun and the police had not prevailed in having this charge dropped—perhaps had made no effort—he was found in technical violation of the terms of an existing parole and was required to return to jail for ninety days.

According to Ranger sources, the Disciples had successfully entered the Ranger area in July and had fired on Rangers without noticeable or effective police intervention.

Mr. Zelkovich did not begin an effort to disarm the Disciples on July 5.

The meeting to review the performance of the parties to the disarmament was convened by First Church representatives on August 3. All parties to the original agreement were represented. In contrast to the June 28 meeting, when First Church representatives had played a mediating and facilitating role, at the August 3 meeting the pastor of First Church convened and conducted the meeting. He opened the meeting with a presentation of agreement terms which had been honored and those which had not been honored. In testimony later given before the Presbytery of Chicago's Special Investigating Committee he recalled the presentation in these words:

I said that the Rangers had lived up to their part of the agreement; that both police and federal officials on the scene July 4th had agreed that this was a substantial disarmament. That was point one.

Point two: the police had promised additional protection on Woodlawn Avenue and it had been reported to me that, if anything, protection had been diminished rather than increased; that the shotgun case had been continued and that Mr. Hairston had been picked up for a parole violation, the violation being that he had—was in illegal possession of a shotgun and the case was continued on that date, so, far from doing what they could in that court situation, it seemed plain, at least to the Rangers, that they had done what they could to make sure that Gene Hairston got in jail; the federal presence at that trial had not materialized, and, furthermore, for the information of the federal representatives, I told them of Mr. Zelkovich's word that the day following the Ranger disarmament, he would be immediately at work in the Disciple area, and they said Mr. Zelkovich had gone on vacation on the day following the gun collection.

The law-enforcement officials could not, nor did they attempt to, dispute the presentation. They were in plain default. Various police officers sought to explain what they had done or not done.

If one finds the June 28 meeting improbable, the August 3 meeting will be found to be even more improbable, because police officers later claimed they had come to the meeting for the sole purpose of getting the guns in the safe, and on being refused had left. First Church representatives recall the police were found in open violation of a sincere good-faith agreement, and had no ground to ask for anything except forgiveness, which they did not do, but, instead, left.

In agreeing to let the walk-in safe be used as a neutral, impregnable, and secure storage place for the weapons, First Church representatives did not on June 28 think of the possibility that the police would default. The church was therefore in the position of holding weapons which did not belong to the Rangers anymore, since the Rangers had surrendered them, but could not belong to the police unless the police abided by their promises. It is irritating for the church to have to point out an unforgivable naïveté. On June 28 the church still honored the word of law-enforcement officials.

The police officers at the August 3 meeting have testified before the McClellan Committee that they came to the meeting for the express purpose of getting the guns. They knew, of course, that the safe's combination was known by two First Church employees who would not have been at the meeting unless specifically invited for that exclusive purpose. Thirty days before, these same officers had discovered to their complete satisfaction that only Miss Eggers and Mrs. Jones could open the safe. Perhaps it was the police intention to pick up the guns that night, since First Church representatives at the meeting were not expert in determining inward intention. But had the police directly asked for the guns, as their testimony indicates, the church's response, whatever else they recall it being, would have had to be prefaced with the words, "We can't open the safe," and these words do not appear in their testimony.

The police later claimed to the press and testified at the McClellan hearings that between August 3 and November 10 they sought on numerous occasions to get the guns, but without success. They claimed the church was adamant. They further claimed that the church said their reason for holding the guns was, "The Rangers might need the guns." One must proceed slowly at such a point. If First Church representatives had been interested in Blackstone Ranger firepower, why would it have made such extensive efforts in late June to facilitate a Ranger disarmament? The fact that some weapons were safely stored and out of Ranger hands permanently is ample warrant to consider the impossibility of the response police officers have *testified* the church made on numerous (non-) occasions when it was requested to turn over the guns. There were no historical occasions on which the police requested or demanded or required the guns between July 4 and November 10. The police testimony pictures the church as being at the least ambivalent and at the most unbalanced in its wildly fluctuating responses to the gun question.

The inherent consistency and believability of the police testimony suffers a great pressure—perhaps a pressure sufficient to shatter it—in the search warrant which they displayed when they entered the church building on November 10. That warrant was not issued on the grounds that First Church had repeatedly refused police requests to rescue the guns from its safe. The search warrant was issued because of information "informants" had furnished. The language of the warrant, and police statements to the press made after the raid, suggested clearly that it was by way of "informants" the police had come upon information about the guns in the safe. Yet before the McClellan Committee the same officers testified under oath that on numerous occasions during the period August 3 to November 10 they had requested the guns and had been refused. The police want it both ways. They knew about the guns and the church refused to let them go, but they had just heard about the guns through informants so they decided they had better arm themselves with a warrant, notify the press, and storm into the church to get the offensive weapons.

The believability of police testimony suffers further pressure when statements made to the press are compared. Sgt. Neal Wilson, who participated as a representative of the Chicago Police Department in all phases of the July 4 gun collection, is quoted in the *Chicago Tribune,* November 11, as saying, "The Chicago police department is completely unaware of any arrangements made by representatives of the Blackstone Rangers and the treasury department relative to the confiscated weapons." On that same day First Church representatives presented to the press their understanding of the agreement under which the weapons were in the church safe. First Church spokesmen declared that Sgt. Wilson participated in the collection and signed the inventory.

Reporters who monitored the First Church press conference then asked Sgt. Wilson about that. He replied, according to the November 12 papers, "I was involved in the situation only after it was set up by the alcohol and tax division of the treasury department. When I left [the church], Zelkovich was still there and the weapons were on a table in the second floor office. I did not see them placed in a safe." Within twenty-four hours Sgt. Wilson had changed his position from being "completely unaware" to "I was involved in the situation only after . . ." With that statement, Sgt. Wilson destroyed the grounds for the warrant which had been issued on the basis of information provided by "informants" not by his own eyes.

Obviously, the inventory becomes a crucial item. And, one may well suppose, its importance was apparent to the officials who conducted the raid on November 10. When the money safe was opened and the envelope with the combination and inventory was located, the assistant corporation counsel for the City of Chicago reached into the envelope and confiscated the inventory. First Church staff, lawyers from the A.C.L.U., an attorney retained by the church at that time (Mr. Lawrence Kennon), and members of the governing board of the church all watched Assistant Corporation Counsel Moridan take the inventory. He did not provide a receipt for it as he did provide a receipt for the confiscated weapons. Hence, when the church sought to present its side to the press on November 11 and 12, it was placed at a remarkable disadvantage. It was in the position of describing an intricate and improbable deal. It was saying the police were well aware of the presence of the guns because police representatives, notably Sgt. Neal Wilson, had placed the guns in the safe themselves and had signed an inventory. Where was the inventory? The assistant corporation counsel for the City of Chicago had confiscated it. The explanation of the missing inventory was as improbable as the story of the deal. Until they could see it, reporters treated the inventory as a "fictitious" inventory. The church had a wild story; the police had the weapons; Mr. Moridan had the inventory.

Three copies of the inventory were made on July 4, 1966. One of those copies has been recovered. It shows clearly the signatures of Sgt. Neal Wilson, Pete Zelkovich, and associate pastor of First Church, Harold Walker. Sgt. Wilson's feigned ignorance of the safe arrangements is simply exploded by the re-emergence of the critical inventory, and his testimony before the McClellan Committee compromised beyond repair.

The final irony does not arise from the eventual appearance of the inventory, which had been so disastrously missing for First Church. The great irony arises on reflection of the police claims that weapons were taken out of the safe, used, replaced, taken out of the safe, used, and replaced—numerous times. This provided the police with their rationale for the raid. The people inside the church might be armed, therefore the police came into the church with their guns drawn. The fact is that none of the weapons in the safe was operable. A .22-caliber rifle had a bent barrel. A .38-caliber pistol was damaged and without a firing mechanism. The "other weapons" were knives, machetes, a seven iron, and assorted other nonfirearms. The safe had all along contained only junk; the federal officials had taken away all of the operating guns.

Some arsenal.

At the time of the raid First Church was concerned to point out the police abuse which occurred when thirty armed and dangerous men stormed into the church building on November 10. These officers wantonly destroyed property throughout the building, although their search warrant restricted them to a second-floor safe. They detained over 100 young people at gun point for over two hours. They arrested guests of the church who were attending a meeting when the raid occurred. (They were later released.) They verbally abused church officers, staff, and attorney Kennon. The church's anger over this mistreatment was more prominently reported than its attempt to present a plausible account of improbable meetings and a bizarre disarmament in July. The police version prevailed. Police spokesmen plastered First Church with a notoriety from which it has not to this day recovered. It is still known as the "Arsenal for the Blackstone Rangers."

73 74 75 76 77 10 9 8 7 6 5 4 3 2 1